THE BOOK OF SAINTS
THE EARLY ERA

AL TRUESDALE, Editor

BEACON HILL PRESS
OF KANSAS CITY

Receive from me things, not clever, but weighty—words,
not decked up to charm a popular audience with cultivated rhetoric,
but simple and fitted by their unvarnished truth
for the proclamation of the divine mercy.
—Cyprian, Bishop of Carthage, *Letter to Donatus*

CONTENTS

INTRODUCTION	7
THE APOSTOLIC FATHERS	11
Clement of Rome	12
The *Teaching of the Twelve Apostles* (*Didache*)	23
Ignatius of Antioch	30
Polycarp of Smyrna	36
The *Shepherd of Hermas*	46
The *Epistle to Diognetus* (*Mathetes*)	52
THE GREEK APOLOGISTS	63
Aristides	65
Justin Martyr	72
Athenagoras	83
Theophilus of Antioch	92
THE "SCHOOL" OF ALEXANDRIA	101
Clement of Alexandria	103
Origen	117
Dionysius of Alexandria	129
THE CHURCH IN THE WEST	135
Irenaeus	137
Hippolytus of Rome	160
Tertullian	166
Cyprian of Carthage	176
THE EASTERN CHURCH AFTER ORIGEN AND BEFORE NICAEA	207
Gregory of Neocaesarea	210
Methodius of Olympus	212
APPENDIX	221
A List of the Ante-Nicene Fathers	221
SOURCES	223

INTRODUCTION

An unfortunate by-product of our highly mobile society is that too often we don't know our relatives, current and past. Children can grow up having little contact with aunts, uncles, cousins, and grandparents. Friends are essential, but only our families can teach how our lives are grounded in unique and intriguing narratives. Only they can tell how our great-grandparents managed to reach California to escape the wind-ravaged dust bowl of the American prairies early in the twentieth century, or how our enterprising parents fled Vietnam at the end of the Vietnam War, possessing only the clothes on their backs.

My brother and I grew up knowing our father's formal education ended at fourth grade. We later learned that at age twelve, after his mother's death, he was effectively orphaned, even rejected by his mother's sister. In spite of this, he learned a trade that permitted him to provide for our family. Hearing the second part of the story increased our appreciation for our father and had a major impact on our own self-understanding and diligence.

What is true of individual families is also true of our Christian family—our fathers and mothers, our sisters and brothers, in Christ. We can grow richer and stronger by learning from the "great cloud of witnesses" (Heb. 12:1, NIV) who "fought the good fight" of faith (2 Tim. 4:7, NIV) before us. What a legacy to pass on! Having listened to their stories, we come away saying, "Wow! I didn't know that."

The purpose of this book is to sit at the feet of some early church fathers who lived after the apostles and before the first ecumenical (general) church council in Nicaea (AD 325). This time is often referred to as the "subapostolic" period. The earliest ante-Nicene fathers are called the apostolic fathers because of what tradition has claimed about their relationship to the apostles. The second group is known as the apologists. They presented reasoned defenses of the Christian faith to a Greco-Roman audience. After that we turn to the fathers associated with the church in Alexandria, Egypt, and next to the fathers of the church in the West, that is, Gaul, Rome, and North Africa. Finally, two Eastern fathers, Gregory of Neocaesarea (third century) and Methodius (late third and early fourth centuries), will instruct us.

All the ante-Nicene fathers faced the threat of official Roman persecution. Some of them became martyrs. Persecution of the young faith came from many quarters, one of which was state-sponsored persecution that varied in intensity, length, and geographical breadth. There were periods of relative calm. Roughly ten periods of persecution ran their course before the Edict of Milan (AD 313) placed Christianity on an equal footing with other religions. Unofficial opposition came from the Roman populace. Christians were judged to be enemies of social cohesion and the empire's well-being because they refused to participate in pagan religious practices that honeycombed Greco-Roman culture. Pagan religion in all accepted forms supported the supremacy of the empire and recognized the emperor as lord and savior. Christians were accused of everything from sedition to committing lewd acts during their religious services, from causing famine to being responsible for military defeats, and from cannibalism to atheism.

Some ante-Nicene fathers will not be drawn on because their writings do not lend themselves to devotional reading. A brief biographical sketch precedes the selections from each father. A prayer (often a hymn) and Scripture references* for reflection follow each reading. In many instances it has been necessary to paraphrase the public-domain translations.

As values that mark our era become more manifestly pagan, and as Christian "memory" fades from the public square (and sometimes from the church), drinking from the rich wells of apostolic Christianity becomes increasingly practical. How to live holy lives in a pagan world is a golden cord that runs straight through the fathers.

---

*Scripture references in boldface distinguish Scripture verses quoted or paraphrased in the selections and prayers.

THE APOSTOLIC FATHERS

The title Apostolic Fathers is assigned to the earliest Christian writings that appear after the New Testament. They were named in the seventeenth century after their writers, the apostolic fathers, who were believed to have known the apostles. In a couple instances, this might have been true. Over time, simply because of the way scholars classified the material, the number of these fathers has grown from five to eight. There is disagreement over how to classify the *Epistle to Diognetus*. With the exception of *Diognetus*, the works of the apostolic fathers are addressed to other Christians. In some instances we can identify the author of a work; in others we know only the name of the document. Some writings of the apostolic fathers are clearly beneficial for edification; some are considerably less so.

CLEMENT OF ROME

In the apostolic father known as Clement of Rome (ca. AD 30–100), we encounter one marked by the spirit of the apostles. He had a clear understanding of the gospel, a love for God and the church, and a passion for order and harmony in Christ's body. Clement had probably known the apostle Paul. He seems to have been at Philippi (ca. AD 57) when Paul was there. Along with godly women and others, Clement "struggled beside [Paul] in the work of the gospel" (Phil. 4:3, NRSV).

He was a copresbyter or clergy with Linus and Cletus in the church at Rome. After the deaths of Linus and Cletus, who were probably martyred under Emperor Nero (ca. AD 64-67), Clement became bishop of Rome. During the latter part of his life, the church in Corinth was plagued by internal conflict. Rebellion by some younger members against the bishop (pastor) had erupted. A "few rash and self-confident persons" had kindled a "pitch of frenzy" (Clement, *First Epistle to the Corinthians,* chap. 1). The turmoil was subverting the faith of many, discouraging others, giving rise to doubt, and generally causing grief.

On behalf of the church in Rome, Clement wrote a letter (ca. AD 96) to the Corinthians. The letter is known as *1 Clement* and also as *The First Epistle of Clement to the Corinthians.* It is a letter sent from one church to another. Its tone and the condition of the Corinthian church remind us of problems Paul addressed decades earlier. In fact, Clement urges the Corinthian Christians to "take up the epistle of the blessed apostle Paul" (chap. 47). Like Paul, Clement appeals for unity, peace, and righteousness in Christ's church. The tone is collegial and commendatory but also firm in its call for reform and correction. Clement tells the congregation that the Christian life must be lived in godly fear before the Lord. His instructions rely heavily on Scripture. The letter was highly esteemed in the early church for its sound doctrine. A second epistle to the Corinthians bears Clement's name but is not considered authentic.

1

Let us yield obedience to God's excellent and glorious will; and imploring his mercy and loving-kindness, while we forsake all fruitless labors and strife and envy that lead to death, let us turn and have recourse to his compassions. Let us steadfastly contemplate those who have perfectly ministered to his excellent glory. Let us take for instance Enoch, who, being found righteous in obedience, was translated; death was never known to happen to him. Noah, being found faithful, preached regeneration to the world, and by him the Lord saved the animals that, with one accord, entered the ark.

CLEMENT, *First Epistle to the Corinthians*, CHAP. 10

Raise us up, O God, by your grace. Let us dedicate ourselves to you through Jesus Christ. We pray for those who are newly converted that they may be strengthened in the faith and that all your people may be mutually comforted by one another. Sanctify us body and soul; grant us the favor to be "made pure from all filthiness of flesh and spirit." May we obtain the good things laid up for us. Do not account any of us unworthy; but be our comforter, helper, and protector, through your Christ, with whom glory, honor, praise, doxology, and thanksgiving be to you and to the Holy Spirit forever. Amen.

CLEMENTINE LITURGY (LATE FOURTH CENTURY),
IN *Constitutions of the Holy Apostles*, BK. 8, SEC. 2.13

FOR REFLECTION: Gen. 5:21-24; 1 Sam. 12:19-25; 2 Cor. 6:6; 7:1; Eph. 4:7-16, 25-32; Phil. 4:4-8; Heb. 11:1-38

2

Having so many great and glorious examples of humility and godly submission set before us, let us turn again to the practice of that peace that from the beginning was the mark set before us. Let us look steadfastly to the Father and Creator of the universe and hold fast to his mighty and surpassingly great gifts and benefits of peace. Let us contemplate him with our understanding and look with the eyes of our soul to his long-suffering will. Let us reflect how free from wrath he is toward all his creation.

CLEMENT, *FIRST EPISTLE TO THE CORINTHIANS*, CHAP. 19

YOU, LORD, remember not every sin of your servants and handmaids, but purify us with the purification of your truth; and direct our steps that we may walk in holiness of heart and do what is good and well-pleasing in your sight. Let us be submissive to your almighty and all-excellent name. Amen.

CLEMENT, *FIRST EPISTLE TO THE CORINTHIANS*, CHAP. 60, LIGHTFOOT

FOR REFLECTION: Deut. 7:7-11; Ezra 9:5-9; Pss. 66:1-20; 95:1-5; Isa. 55:7-9; Eph. 2:4-7; Heb. 4:12-16; 12:1-3

3

The heavens, revolving under God's government, are subject to him in peace. Day and night they run the course appointed by him, in no wise hindering each other. The sun and moon, with the companies of stars, roll on in harmony according to his command within their prescribed limits and without any deviation. The fruitful earth, according to his will, brings forth food in abundance at the proper seasons for humans and beasts and all other living beings. The seasons of spring, summer, autumn, and winter peacefully give place to each other. God does good to all but most abundantly to us who have fled for refuge to his compassions through Jesus Christ our Lord, to whom be glory and majesty forever and ever. Amen.

CLEMENT, *First Epistle to the Corinthians*, CHAP. 20

O Lord, make your face to shine on us for good, in peace, that we may be shielded by your mighty hand and delivered from every sin by your uplifted arm. We are submissive to your almighty and all-excellent name. Amen.

CLEMENT, *First Epistle to the Corinthians,* CHAP. 60, LIGHTFOOT

FOR REFLECTION: Job 38:4-11; Pss. 8:1-9; 19:1-4; 24:1-2; Isa. 40:12-17; Jer. 10:12-16; John 1:1-19; Col. 1:15-20

4

Take heed, beloved, lest God's many kindnesses lead to the condemnation of us all. For thus it will be unless we walk worthy of him and, with one mind, do those things that are good and well-pleasing in his sight. Let us consider how near he is and that none of the thoughts or reasonings in which we engage are hid from him. Let us reverence the Lord Jesus Christ, whose blood was given for us; let us esteem those who have the rule over us; let us honor the aged among us; let us train up the young in the fear of God. Let your children be partakers of true Christian training; let them learn how important humility is for God—how much the spirit of pure affection can prevail with him—how excellent and great is a holy fear of him, how it saves all those who walk in it with a pure mind. For God is a Searcher of our thoughts and desires; his breath is in us. When he pleases, he will take it away.

CLEMENT, *FIRST EPISTLE TO THE CORINTHIANS*, CHAP. 21

O LORD, give concord and peace to all who dwell on the earth, even as you gave to our fathers when they called on you in faith and truth, submissive as we are to your almighty and all-excellent name. Amen.

CLEMENT, *FIRST EPISTLE TO THE CORINTHIANS*, CHAP. 60, LIGHTFOOT

FOR REFLECTION: Deut. 30:1-20; Isa. 61:8-11; Mic. 6:6-8; Rom. 6:1-23; Eph. 4:17-32; 1 Thess. 5:12-13; Heb. 13:17

5

Having then our Christian hope, let our souls be bound to him who is faithful to his promises and just in his judgments. He who has commanded us not to lie shall much more himself not lie. Nothing is impossible with God except to lie. Let his gift of faith therefore be stirred up within us. By the word of his might, he established all things, and by his word, he can overthrow them. When and as he pleases, he does all things, and none of the things determined by him shall pass away. All things are open before him, and nothing can be hidden from his counsel.

CLEMENT, *FIRST EPISTLE TO THE CORINTHIANS*, CHAP. 27

ALMIGHTY, ETERNAL GOD, *Lord of the whole world, the Creator and Governor of all things, we pray for the peace and happy settlement of the world and of the holy churches. Give us your peace that can never be taken away. May you fulfill in us such virtue as is in keeping with godliness. We pray for our enemies and those who hate us. We pray for those who persecute us for the name of the Lord, that he may pacify their anger and scatter their wrath. We pray for those who are not yet Christians and for those who have wandered from the way, that the Lord may convert them. We pray for infants in the faith, that the Lord may perfect them in his fear and bring them to complete maturity. We pray for our sisters and brothers in Christ, that the Lord may keep us all and preserve us to the end by grace. Deliver us, O Lord, from the evil one, from all the scandals of those who work iniquity. Preserve us for your heavenly kingdom. Save us, and lift us up, O God, by your mercy. May we give ourselves and each other to the living God, through Jesus Christ. Amen.*

CLEMENTINE LITURGY (LATE FOURTH CENTURY),
IN *CONSTITUTIONS OF THE HOLY APOSTLES*, BK. 8, SEC. 2.9, 10

FOR REFLECTION: Pss. 19:1-3; 31:1-15; 138:2; Isa. 51:6-8; Matt. 24:35; Rom. 8:18-39; 2 Cor. 1:18-22; Titus 1:2; Heb. 6:18; 10:22-37; 11:18-29

6

Seeing, therefore, that we belong to the Holy One, let us do those things that pertain to holiness, avoiding all evil speaking, all abominable and impure attachments, together with all drunkenness, all abominable lusts, detestable adultery, and abhorrent pride. "For God," says the Scripture, "resists the proud, but gives grace to the humble." Let us cling, then, to those to whom grace has been given by God. Let us clothe ourselves with peace and humility, ever exercising self-control, standing far off from all whispering and evil speaking, being known by our works and not our words. Let our praise be to God and not to ourselves, for God rejects those that commend themselves. Let testimony to our good deeds be borne by others, as it was in the case of our righteous forefathers. Boldness, arrogance, and audacity belong to those who are accursed of God; but moderation, humility, and meekness belong to such as are blessed by him.

We, being called by God's will in Christ Jesus, are not justified by ourselves, by our own wisdom, understanding, or godliness, or by works we have performed in holiness of heart but by that faith through which, from the beginning, Almighty God has justified his people. To him be glory forever and ever. Amen.

CLEMENT, *First Epistle to the Corinthians*, CHAPS. 30, 32

We praise you, we sing hymns to you, we bless you for your great glory, O Lord our King, the Father of Christ the immaculate Lamb, who takes away the sin of the world. Praise becomes you, hymns become you, and glory becomes you, the God and Father, through the Son, in the most Holy Spirit, forever and ever. Amen.

"Daily Prayers," in *Constitutions of the Holy Apostles*, BK. 7, SEC. 5.48

FOR REFLECTION: Prov. 3:34; Eph. 1:4-14; 4:20-24; Phil. 1:10-11; 2:15; 4:8; Col. 3:5-15; **James 4:6; 1 Pet. 5:5**

7

Let us hasten with all energy and readiness of mind to perform every good work. For the Creator and Lord of all rejoices in his works. By his infinitely great power he established the heavens, and by his incomprehensible wisdom he adorned them. He also divided the earth from the water that surrounds it and fixed it on an immoveable foundation. The animals also that are on it he commanded into existence by his own word. Above all, with his holy and undefiled hands he formed humans, the most excellent of his creatures. They are truly great because of the understanding God gave them. They are the express likeness of his image. Having thus finished all these things, God approved them, blessed them, and said, "Increase and multiply." We see, then, how all righteous people have been adorned with good works and how the Lord himself, adorning himself with his works, rejoiced. Having therefore such an example, let us without delay obey his will, and let us work the work of righteousness with our whole strength.

CLEMENT, First Epistle to the Corinthians, CHAP. 33

Breathe in us, O our Lord and God, the fragrance of the sweetness of your love; illumined are our souls through the knowledge of your truth: may we be rendered worthy of receiving the manifestation of your Beloved in the holy heavens where we will give thanks to you. In the meantime, we will glorify you without ceasing in your church, which is crowned and filled with every aid and blessing. You are Lord and Father, Creator of all. Amen.

Adaeus and Maris, The Liturgy of the Blessed Apostles (ca. AD 150)

FOR REFLECTION: Gen. 1:26-28; Exod. 20:1-17; Rom. 12:1-21; Col. 3:5-17; Rev. 22:12-21

8

How blessed and wonderful, beloved, are the gifts of God! Life in immortality, splendor in righteousness, truth in perfect confidence, faith in assurance, self-control in holiness! And all these are ours now. What then shall those things be that are prepared for those who wait for Christ's coming? The Creator and Father of all worlds, the Most Holy, alone knows their measure and their beauty. Let us therefore earnestly strive to be found in the number of those who wait for him, so that we may share in his promised gifts. But how, beloved, can this be accomplished? Only if our understanding is fixed by faith in God; if we earnestly seek the things that are pleasing and acceptable to him; if we do the things that are in harmony with his blameless will; and if we follow the way of truth, casting away all unrighteousness and iniquity, along with all covetousness, strife, evil practices, deceit, whispering, and evil speaking, all hatred of God, pride and haughtiness, and all vainglory and sinful ambition.

CLEMENT, FIRST EPISTLE TO THE CORINTHIANS, CHAP. 35

ENLIGHTEN, O OUR LORD AND GOD, our meditations to hear and understand your life-giving and divine commands in the Epistles. Grant to us through your grace and mercy to gather from them the assurance of your love, hope, and salvation suitable to soul and body. We shall sing to you everlasting glory without ceasing, O Lord of all. Amen.

ADAEUS AND MARIS, THE LITURGY OF THE BLESSED APOSTLES (CA. AD 150)

✦✦✦

FOR REFLECTION: Pss. 27:1-5; 31:1-3; Rom. 12:1-2; Eph. 4:17-32; Heb. 10:32-39; 12:29; 1 Pet. 1:3-21

9

Let him who loves Christ keep his commandments. Who can describe the blessed bond of God's love? What person is able to tell the excellence of its beauty as it ought to be told? The height to which love exalts is unspeakable. Love unites us to God. Love covers a multitude of sins. Love bears all things, is long-suffering in all things. There is nothing base, nothing arrogant, in love. Love admits of no schisms; love gives rise to no seditions; love does all things in harmony. By God's love have all his elect been made perfect; without love nothing is well-pleasing to God. In love has the Lord gathered us to himself. Because of the love he has for us, Jesus Christ our Lord gave his blood for us by the will of the Father; his flesh for our flesh, and his soul for our souls.

CLEMENT, *FIRST EPISTLE TO THE CORINTHIANS*, CHAP. 49

IN PEACE LET US BESEECH THE LORD. For the peace that is from above, for God's love to humankind, and for the salvation of our souls, let us beseech the Lord. For the peace of the whole world and for the unity of all the holy churches of God, let us beseech the Lord. For the remission of our sins, and forgiveness of our transgressions, and for our deliverance from all tribulation, wrath, danger, and distress, and from the uprising of our enemies, let us beseech the Lord. Amen.

THE DIVINE LITURGY OF JAMES THE HOLY APOSTLE (CA. AD 150–200)

FOR REFLECTION: Matt. 5:43-48; 19:16-22; John 17:1-26; 1 Cor. 13:1-13; 14:1; Heb. 13:1-22; James 1:27; 5:20; 1 Pet. 4:8; 1 John 4:7-21

10

You see, beloved, how great and wonderful a thing love is, and that there is no declaring its perfection. Who is fit to be found in it, except such as God has granted to become so? Let us pray, therefore, and implore his mercy that we may live blameless in love, free from all human partialities for one above another. All the generations from Adam even to this day have passed away; but those who through the grace of God have been made perfect in love now possess a place among the godly. They will be manifest at the consummation of the kingdom of Christ. Blessed are we, beloved, if we keep the commandments of God in the harmony of love, that so through love our sins may be forgiven. "Blessed are they whose transgressions are forgiven, and whose sins are covered." This blessedness comes upon those who have been chosen by God through Jesus Christ our Lord; to whom be glory forever and ever. Amen.

CLEMENT, *First Epistle to the Corinthians*, CHAP. 50

May God, who sees all things, and who is the Ruler of all spirits and the Lord of all flesh—who chose our Lord Jesus Christ and us through him to be a peculiar people—grant to every soul that calls upon his glorious and holy name faith, fear, peace, patience, long-suffering, self-control, purity, and sobriety, to the well-pleasing of his name, through our High Priest and Protector, Jesus Christ, by whom be to him glory, majesty, power, and honor, both now and forevermore. Amen.

CLEMENT, *First Epistle to the Corinthians*, CHAP. 58

FOR REFLECTION: Ps. 32:1-2; Isa. 26:20; Luke 10:25-37; Eph. 5:21-33; 1 Thess. 5:8-14; Heb. 13:1-6; 1 John 3:11-24

THE *TEACHING OF THE TWELVE APOSTLES* (*DIDACHE*)

The *Teaching of the Twelve Apostles*, also known as the *Didache* (Greek, *didachē* [teaching]), is one of the earliest Christian writings not included in the New Testament. Its ancient title was the *Lord's Teaching through the Twelve Apostles to the Nations*. The *Didache* was quoted or mentioned by numerous early Christian writers such as Clement of Alexandria, Origen, Athanasius, and the church historian Eusebius. A few fathers even held it to be inspired and as belonging to the New Testament. The *Didache* in its final form is the result of combining earlier sources that cannot be precisely identified. It reflects life in the church perhaps as early as AD 70. It probably achieved its final form about AD 150.

The *Didache*'s sixteen chapters are divided into three parts (scholars disagree over the number of parts). The *first part* (chaps. 1–5) contains teaching on the "two ways" (or "two paths"). One "way" leads to life, and the other to death. This part of the *Didache* is found in other early Christian writings and seems to have existed independently at one time. This section summarizes the Christian's life and seems to have been intended for catechumens (persons being prepared for baptism). The *second part* (chaps. 6–14) is a manual of instruction for church order and practice. It contains warnings against false teachers, instructions for baptism, fasting, the Lord's Prayer, and prayers for a community meal, the exact identity of which is not clear. Chapters 9 and 10 speak of a meal in which the communicants "eat their fill," while chapter 14 speaks of a meal that occurs on the Lord's Day and is considered a "sacrifice." The *third part* of the *Didache* (chaps. 15–16) is a manual of instruction on offices and positions of church leadership. It ends with an appeal to watch and prepare for the Lord's return.

11

There are two ways, one of life and one of death, but a great difference between the two ways. The way of life, then, is this: first, you shall love God who made you; second, love your neighbor as yourself, and do not do to another what you would not want done to you. And of these sayings the teaching is this: bless those who curse you, and pray for your enemies, and fast for those who persecute you. For what reward is there for loving those who love you? Do not the Gentiles the same? But love those who hate you, and you shall not have an enemy. Abstain from fleshly and worldly lusts. If someone strikes your right cheek, turn to him the other also, and you shall be perfect. If someone forces you to go one mile, go with him two. If someone takes your cloak, give him also your coat. If someone takes from you what is yours, ask it not back, for indeed you are not able. Give to everyone who asks you, and ask it not back; for the Father wills that to all should be given of our own blessings (free gifts). Happy is the person who gives according to the commandment, for he is guiltless. Woe to the one who receives but has no need. If one receives who has need, he is guiltless; but he who receives and has no need will pay the penalty.

DIDACHE, CHAP. 1

TRULY IT IS BECOMING AND RIGHT, proper and due, to praise you, to sing of you, to bless you, to worship you, to glorify you, to give you thanks—Maker of all things, the Treasure of eternal good things, the Fountain of life and immortality, God and Lord of all. Amen.

THE DIVINE LITURGY OF JAMES THE HOLY APOSTLE (CA. AD 150–200)

FOR REFLECTION: Lev. 26:1-46; Deut. 5:1-33; Prov. 23:27-32; Isa. 33:15-17; Ezek. 18:21-24; Matt. 5:13-48; Phil. 3:7-16

12

The second commandment of the teaching: You shall not commit murder; you shall not commit adultery; you shall not commit pederasty; you shall not commit fornication; you shall not steal; you shall not practice magic; you shall not practice witchcraft; you shall not murder a child by abortion, nor kill one that has been born. You shall not covet the possessions of your neighbor; you shall not swear; you shall not bear false witness; you shall not speak evil; you shall bear no grudge. You shall neither be double-minded nor double-tongued, for to be double-tongued is a snare of death. Your speech shall neither be false nor empty but fulfilled by deed. You shall be neither covetous nor rapacious nor a hypocrite nor disposed to evil nor haughty. You shall not take evil counsel against your neighbor. You shall not hate any person; but some you shall reprove, for some you shall pray, and some you shall love more than your own life.

DIDACHE, CHAP. 2

TRULY IT IS BECOMING AND RIGHT, proper and due, to praise you whom the heavens praise, and all the host of them; the sun, the moon, and all the choir of the stars; the earth, sea, and all that is in them; Jerusalem, the heavenly assembly, and church of the firstborn that are written in heaven; spirits of just men and of prophets; souls of martyrs and apostles; angels, archangels, thrones, dominions, principalities, authorities, and dread powers; and the many-eyed cherubim and the six-winged seraphim, who with loud voices sing the victorious hymn of your majestic glory, crying aloud, praising, shouting, and saying: "Holy, holy, holy, O Lord of Sabaoth, the heaven and the earth are full of your glory. Hosanna in the highest; blessed is he who comes in the name of the Lord. Hosanna in the highest." Amen.

THE DIVINE LITURGY OF JAMES THE HOLY APOSTLE (CA. AD 150–200)

FOR REFLECTION: Lev. 11:44-45; Ps. 24:3-5; Isa. 35:3-10; Col. 3:5-17; Titus 1:10-16; James 1:20; 5:1-11; Jude vv. 1-23

13

My child, flee from every evil thing and from every likeness of it. Be not prone to anger, for anger leads to murder. Be neither jealous nor quarrelsome nor of a hot temper, for out of all these, murders are born. My child, do not be a lustful person, for lust leads to fornication. Be neither a filthy talker nor of lofty eye, for out from all these, adulteries are born. My child, do not lie, since a lie leads to theft. Be neither money-loving nor boastful, for out of all these, thefts are born. My child, do not be a grumbler, since it leads to blasphemy. Be neither self-centered nor evil-minded, for out of all these, blasphemies are engendered. Instead, be meek, since the meek shall inherit the earth. Be long-suffering, merciful, guileless, gentle, and good. You shall neither exalt yourself nor give excessive confidence to your soul. Your soul shall not be joined to arrogant people, but with the just and humble shall you associate.

DIDACHE, CHAP. 3

WE THANK YOU, HOLY FATHER, for your holy name, which you caused to tabernacle in our hearts, and for the knowledge, faith, and immortality that you made known to us through Jesus your Servant. To you be glory forever. Amen.

DIDACHE, CHAP. 10

FOR REFLECTION: Prov. 11:2-8; Hos. 10:12; Matt. 5:1-16; John 14:21-24; 15:4-12; Rom. 15:1-18

14

Do not long for division but rather bring to peace those who are contentious. Judge righteously, and do not have regard for persons when you reprove of transgressions. Do not stretch out your hands to receive and then draw them back when you should give. Do not turn away from one who is in need; rather, share all things with your brother or sister, and do not say that your possessions are your own. For if you are partakers in that which is immortal, how much more in things that are mortal? Teach your son or daughter the fear of God from his or her youth. You shall hate all hypocrisy and everything not pleasing to the Lord. Do not in any way forsake the commandments of the Lord, but keep what you have received, neither adding to them nor taking away. In the church you shall acknowledge your transgressions, and you shall not approach prayer with an evil conscience. This is the way of life.

DIDACHE, CHAP. 4

O LORD ALMIGHTY, THE MOST HIGH, who dwells on high, you are the Holy One that rests among the saints, eternal, the only King, who through Christ has given us knowledge of the gospel. We acknowledge your glory and name, which Christ revealed to us for our understanding. Do now through Christ look down on us and deliver us from all ignorance and wicked practice. Grant that we may fear you in earnest, love you with affection, and have a due reverence for your glory. Be gracious and merciful to us, and harken to us when we pray. Preserve us, that we may be unmovable, blameless, and without reproach, that we may be holy in body and spirit, not having spot or wrinkle or any such thing, but that we may be complete in you. Amen.

CLEMENTINE LITURGY (LATE FOURTH CENTURY),
IN *CONSTITUTIONS OF THE HOLY APOSTLES*, BK. 8, SEC. 2.11

FOR REFLECTION: Amos 8:4-10; Mic. 6:6-8; Matt. 5:21–7:27; John 17:1-26; Rom. 14:17-19; Eph. 4:1-7; James 1:2–2:26; 3:13-18; 1 John 3:11-22

15

The way of death is this: First of all it is evil and accursed: murders, adultery, lust, fornication, thefts, idolatries, magic arts, witchcrafts, rape, false witness, hypocrisy, double-mindedness, deceit, haughtiness, depravity, self-will, greediness, filthy talking, jealousy, arrogance, self-elevation, boastfulness; persecutors of the good, hating truth, loving a lie, not seeking the reward of righteousness, not clinging to the good or to righteous judgment, being alert, not for what is good, but for what is evil. From such persons meekness and endurance are far removed. They love vanities, pursue revenge, are not merciful to the poor, do not labor for the afflicted, and do not know him who created them. They murder children, destroying the handiwork of God. They turn away from the needy, afflicting the one who is distressed. They are advocates for the rich, lawless judges against the poor. They are utter sinners. Be delivered, children, from all such persons.

Didache, CHAP. 5

Remember, Lord, your Church, to deliver it from all evil and to make it perfect in your love. Gather it from the four winds, sanctified for your kingdom, which you have prepared for your church, for yours is the power and the glory forever. Amen.

Didache, CHAP. 10

FOR REFLECTION: Ps. 112:1-10; Isa. 33:15-17; James 1:22-25; 1 John 2:15-29

16

If anyone comes and teaches you the entire yoke of the Lord, receive him. But if the teacher turns and teaches a destructive doctrine, hear him not. If he teaches so as to increase righteousness and knowledge of the Lord, receive him as you would receive the Lord. But concerning the apostles and prophets, act according to the decree of the gospel. Let every apostle who comes to you be received as the Lord. A true prophet holds to the ways of the Lord. Therefore by their conduct shall the false prophet and the true prophet be distinguished. Receive everyone who comes in the name of the Lord, but prove and know them well; for you shall have understanding to the right and to the left.

DIDACHE, CHAPS. 6, 11–12

O GOD ALMIGHTY, the true God, to whom nothing can be compared, who is everywhere and who is present in all things, be gracious to us and hear us for your name's sake. Bless those that bow before you, and grant the petitions of their hearts. Reject none of them from your kingdom, but sanctify, guard, cover, and assist them. Deliver your people from the adversary and every enemy. Keep their households and guard "their comings in and their goings out." For to you belongs glory, praise, majesty, worship, and adoration and to your Son Jesus, your Christ, our Lord and God and King, and to the Holy Spirit, forever and ever. Amen.

CLEMENTINE LITURGY (LATE FOURTH CENTURY),
IN *CONSTITUTIONS OF THE HOLY APOSTLES*, BK. 8, SEC. 2.15

FOR REFLECTION: Ps. 121:1-8; Isa. 26:3-4; 40:28-31; 43:10-21; Matt. 25:34-46; Luke 14:12-14; 1 Pet. 4:9-11; 1 John 4:1-12

IGNATIUS OF ANTIOCH

To sit at the feet of Ignatius of Antioch (ca. AD 50–ca. 98–117), also called Theophorus (God-bearer), is to be instructed by a sterling Christian pastor whose love for Christ and the church breathes the air of the New Testament. It is quite possible he and his friend Polycarp had known and listened to the apostle John. The endearing tradition that Ignatius was the child that Jesus set forth as a model for entering the kingdom of God (Matt. 18:2-6) is without basis, except that it shows Ignatius's nearness to apostolic times.

In Antioch Ignatius was arrested and condemned to be devoured by wild beasts in Rome. Persecution of Christians in Syria had broken out because Emperor Trajan (r. AD 98–117) decreed that to strengthen the universality of his reign everyone under his authority should worship the Roman deities. Those who refused to obey would face the death penalty. Ignatius valiantly refused to worship the gods and to deny his Christ. He was arrested and hauled before the emperor, who was then in Antioch. Trajan charged Ignatius with refusing to obey the edict and of encouraging others to follow his lead. Condemned to death, Ignatius was sent to Rome on foot. He wrote that he was "chained between ten leopards," ten Roman soldiers "who, even when they receive benefits, show themselves all the worse" (*Epistle to the Romans,* chap. 5). His chains he called his "spiritual jewels" (*Epistle to the Ephesians,* chap. 11).

On the way to Rome, Ignatius received delegations from churches in Asia Minor. He in turn wrote letters to the churches, seven in all. The letters provide a window into the young Christian church in Syria and Asia Minor at the beginning of the second century. There are actually fifteen letters that bear Ignatius's name, but only seven are believed authentic. Four of the seven were written from Smyrna to the Ephesians, the Magnesians, the Trallians, and the Romans. Three were written from Troas to Smyrna; Polycarp, the bishop of Smyrna; and Philadelphia. Reading the epistles brings one as near to the spirit of the New Testament as any early Christian writings. Regrettably, there aren't as many "devotional" sections as we might like.

In his letters, Ignatius has absolutely no reservation about dying for his Lord. He asks the Ephesians not to pray for deliverance from "fighting with beasts at Rome" and appeals to the Roman Christians that they not to try to prevent him from becoming "food for the wild beasts." His riveting preoccupation is for the well-being of Christ's church. Ignatius is concerned about persecution from outside the church and about false teachers who harm the church from within. The counsel Ignatius offers is as lively and applicable today as it was for the young second-century church. Above all, Ignatius wants to be assured of order and unyielding faith in the churches. He is a shepherd who will soon be forcibly removed from Jesus' flock. He is far more interested in their well-being than in his. In particular, in such dangerous times the church in Syria is now without episcopal leadership. Ignatius's letter to Polycarp, his dear friend who will soon walk the path to martyrdom, is especially inspiring.

17

I have heard of some who taught false doctrine among you. But you stopped your ears, that you might not receive those things sown by them. You are stones of the temple of the Father, prepared for the building of God the Father and drawn up on high by the instrument of Jesus Christ, which is the cross, making use of the Holy Spirit as a rope, while your faith was the means by which you ascended and your love was the way leading up to God. You, therefore, as well as all your fellow travelers, are God-bearers, temple-bearers, Christ-bearers, bearers of holiness, adorned in all respects with the commandments of Jesus Christ, in whom also I exult that I have been thought worthy, by means of this epistle, to converse and rejoice with you, because with respect to your Christian life, you love nothing but God only.

IGNATIUS, *EPISTLE TO THE EPHESIANS*, CHAP. 9

COME, HOLY GHOST, our hearts inspire,
Let us your influence prove,
Source of the old prophetic fire,
Fountain of light and love.

. . . .

Expand your wings, celestial Dove,
Brood o'er our nature's night;
On our disordered spirits move,
And let there now be light. Amen.

A COLLECTION OF HYMNS FOR THE USE OF THE PEOPLE CALLED METHODISTS (1889), HYMN 87

FOR REFLECTION: John 12:32; Col. 3:12-17; 1 Thess. 4:1-12; 1 Pet. 2:1-12; 2 Pet. 1:1-21

18

Pray without ceasing on behalf of others. For there is in them hope of repentance, that they may attain to God. See, then, that they be instructed by your works, if in no other way. Be meek in response to their wrath, humble in opposition to their boasting: to their blasphemies return your prayers; in contrast to their error, be steadfast in the faith; and for their cruelty, manifest your gentleness. While we take care not to imitate their conduct, let us be found their brethren in all true kindness; and let us seek to be followers of the Lord (who was ever more unjustly treated, more destitute, more condemned?) so that no plant of the devil may be found in you, but you may remain in all holiness and sobriety in Jesus Christ, both with respect to the flesh and the spirit.

IGNATIUS, *EPISTLE TO THE EPHESIANS*, CHAP. 10

JOYFUL, JOYFUL, WE ADORE THEE,
God of glory, Lord of love;
Hearts unfold like flow'rs before thee,
Opening to the sun above.
Melt the clouds of sin and sadness;
Drive the dark of doubt away.
Giver of immortal gladness,
Fill us with the light of day! Amen.

HENRY VAN DYKE (1852–1933), STTL, NO. 17

FOR REFLECTION: Num. 7:3; Ps. 34:1-10; Isa. 57:15; Jer. 8:4; Matt. 5:4, 13-16; Gal. 5:22; Col. 1:21-23; 2 Tim. 2:24-25; James 3:17; Rev. 2:8-11

19

Come together often as the church to give thanks to God and to show forth his praise. When we assemble frequently in the same place, the powers of Satan are destroyed, and the destruction at which he aims is prevented by the unity of your faith. Nothing is more precious than peace, by which all war, both in heaven and earth, is brought to an end.

None of these things is hid from you, if ye perfectly possess that faith and a love for Christ Jesus that is the beginning and end of life. The beginning is faith, and the end is love. Now these two, being inseparable, are of God. All other things required for a holy life follow after them. No person who truly makes a profession of faith continues to sin. Nor does a person who possesses love hate anyone. The tree is manifest by its fruit; so that those who profess to be Christians should be recognized by their conduct. There is no request for a mere profession. The need is that a person continue to live in the power of faith to the end.

IGNATIUS, *EPISTLE TO THE EPHESIANS*, CHAPS. 13–14

I WANT A PRINCIPLE WITHIN
Of jealous, godly fear,
A sensibility of sin,
A pain to feel it near;
I want the first approach to feel
Of pride, or fond desire,
To catch the wandering of my will,
And quench the kindling fire. Amen.

A COLLECTION OF HYMNS FOR THE USE OF THE PEOPLE CALLED METHODISTS (1889), HYMN 308

FOR REFLECTION: Matt. 12:31-37; Luke 10:27; John 3:1-24; Eph. 6:10-18; 1 Tim 1:14

20

It is better for one to be silent and act like a Christian than to speak and not act like one. It is good to teach if the one who speaks also acts. There was one Teacher who spoke and it was done, while even the things he did in silence were worthy of the Father. He who possesses the word of Jesus is truly able to hear even his silence, so that he may be perfect and may act as he speaks and be recognized by his silence. There is nothing that is hid from God, but our very secrets are near to him. Let us therefore do all things as those who have God dwelling in us, that we may be his temples, and he may be in us as our God, which indeed he is, and will manifest himself before us.

IGNATIUS, *EPISTLE TO THE EPHESIANS*, CHAP. 15

DEAR LORD AND FATHER OF MANKIND,
Forgive our foolish ways!
Reclothe us in our rightful minds;
In purer lives your service find;
In deeper rev'rence, praise.

. . . .

Breathe thro' the heats of our desire
Your coolness and your balm.
Let sense be dumb, let flesh retire;
Speak thro' the earthquake, wind, and fire,
O still, small voice of calm! Amen.

JOHN GREENLEAF WHITTIER (1807-92), STTL, NO. 472

FOR REFLECTION: Ps. 91:1-16; Matt. 5:19; 6:6-18; Rom. 10:9-10; 1 Cor. 5:18-20; 6:9-20; 1 John 3:14—4:21; Jude vv. 20-25

POLYCARP OF SMYRNA

In Polycarp, bishop of Smyrna (modern Izmir, Turkey), we meet one of the most revered leaders of the early church. He is remembered for unwavering fidelity to Jesus Christ and for his defense of sound doctrine against those who would distort it. Polycarp's theological perspective is similar to that found in the gospel of John. The riveting account of Polycarp's martyrdom is another reason he is so revered.

We know little about Polycarp's life. He was the dear and younger friend of Ignatius of Antioch and was martyred after Ignatius. As young men, Polycarp, Ignatius, and Papias may have been pupils of the apostle John. Polycarp had probably come in contact with many who had seen Christ. It is possible he was the "angel of the church in Smyrna" to whom Christ in the book of Revelation said, "Be faithful until death, and I will give you the crown of life" (2:8, 10, NRSV). If so, in martyrdom Polycarp fully obeyed his Lord.

Irenaeus, one of the great early defenders of orthodoxy whom we will meet later, was Polycarp's student. He paints the following picture of his teacher: "I could describe the very place in which the blessed Polycarp sat and taught; his going out and coming in; the whole tenor of his life; his personal appearance; how he would speak of conversations he had held with John and with others who had seen the Lord; how he made mention of their words and of whatever he had heard from them respecting the Lord" (Eusebius, *Ecclesiastical History*, bk. 5, chap. 20, sec. 6).

As Ignatius of Antioch made his way to Rome and to martyrdom, he passed through Smyrna where he spent time with Polycarp. After resuming his journey to Rome, Ignatius addressed a letter to Polycarp from Troas.

After the martyrdom of Ignatius, the church at Philippi (the church the apostle Paul loved so intensely) sent a letter to Polycarp in Smyrna asking him to send to them words of exhortation. They also asked Polycarp to transmit a letter to the church at Antioch written by them. The Philippians asked Polycarp to send to them copies of any of Ignatius's letters in his possession. In addition to sending letters of Ignatius, on behalf of the presbyters then with Polycarp, he sent an exhortation (letter).

After visiting Rome in AD 155, in extreme old age, Polycarp was arrested and martyred, probably in February 156. His martyrdom occurred in the city where he had borne Christian witness as bishop. Shortly after Polycarp's death, the church in Smyrna sent the *Martyrdom of Polycarp* to the church in Philomelium (modern Akşehir, Turkey) and, by circulation, to the whole church. The piece stands as a sterling witness to the power of Christ as manifest in human weakness.

21

Polycarp and the presbyters with him, to the church of God sojourning at Philippi: Mercy be multiplied to you, and peace from God Almighty, and from the Lord Jesus Christ our Savior.

I have greatly rejoiced with you in our Lord Jesus Christ because you have followed the example of true love as displayed by God and have accompanied, as became you, the persecuted who were bound in chains—the fitting ornaments of saints. Those chains are indeed the diadems of the true elect of God and our Lord. The strong root of your faith, spoken of in days gone by, endures even until now. It brings forth fruit to our Lord Jesus Christ, who for our sins suffered death, but "whom God raised from the dead, having loosed the bands of the grave." You, Philippians, "rejoice with joy unspeakable and full of glory" into which many desire to enter. You have been saved by grace and not by works.

POLYCARP, *Epistle to the Philippians*, GREETINGS AND CHAP. 1

GOD,
All my hope on you is founded;
    All my trust you will renew;
Safe through change and chance you guide me,
    Only good and only true:
God unknown,
You alone
Call my heart to be your own. Amen.

JOACHIM NEANDER (1650-80), TRANS. ROBERT SEYMOUR BRIDGES (1899),
HYMNARY

FOR REFLECTION: Acts 2:22-36; Rom. 15:13; Eph. 2:8-9; Phil. 1:5; Col. 1:9-18; **1 Pet. 1:8**

22

Gird up your loins; serve the Lord in fear and in truth as those who have forsaken the vain, empty talk and error of the multitude. You have believed on the Father who raised our Lord Jesus Christ from the dead. The Father gave him glory and a throne at his right hand. To Christ all things in heaven and on earth are subject. Him every spirit serves. He will come as the Judge of the living and the dead. His blood will God require of those who do not believe in him. But the Father who raised Jesus from the dead will raise us also, if we do his will and walk in his commandments, if we love what he loved, keeping ourselves from all unrighteousness, covetousness, love of money, evil speaking, and false witness. Let us not return evil for evil, railing for railing, blow for blow, or cursing for cursing. We must be merciful, that we may obtain mercy.

POLYCARP, *Epistle to the Philippians*, CHAP. 2

We give Thee thanks, yea, more than thanks, O Lord our God, the Father of our Lord and God and Savior Jesus Christ, for all your goodness at all times and in all places, because you have shielded, rescued, helped, and guided us all the days of our lives. We pray and beseech you, merciful God, to grant that by your goodness we may spend all the days of our lives without sin, in fullness of joy, health, safety, holiness, and reverence for you. But all envy, all fear, all temptation, all the influence of Satan, all the snares of wicked people, do, O Lord, drive away from us and from your church, through the grace, mercy, and love of your only begotten Son. Through whom and with whom be glory and power to you, by your most holy, good, and life-giving Spirit, now, henceforth, and forevermore. Amen.

THE DIVINE LITURGY OF THE HOLY APOSTLE AND EVANGELIST MARK
(BEFORE AD 200)

FOR REFLECTION: Ps. 2:11; Matt. 3:10; 6:12-14; 7:1; Luke 6:20, 36; Acts 17:31; Rom. 8:11; 1 Cor. 6:14; 2 Cor. 4:14; Eph. 6:14; Phil. 2:10; 1 Pet. 1:13, 21; 3:22

23

If we entreat the Lord to forgive us, we ought also to forgive, for we are before the eyes of our Lord and God. We must all appear before the judgment seat of Christ and give an account of ourselves. Let us then serve him in fear, and with all reverence, even as he himself has commanded us, and as the apostles who preached the gospel to us, and the prophets who proclaimed beforehand the Lord's coming taught us. Let us be zealous in our pursuit of that which is good.

Anyone who distorts the teachings of the Lord because of his own lusts, and who says there is neither a resurrection nor a judgment, that person is the firstborn of Satan. Forsaking the vanity of many and their false doctrines, let us return to the word that has been handed down to us from the beginning. Let us "watch unto prayer" and persevere in fasting, beseeching in our prayers the all-seeing God "not to lead us into temptation." As the Lord has said, "The spirit truly is willing, but the flesh is weak."

POLYCARP, *EPISTLE TO THE PHILIPPIANS*, CHAPS. 6–7

O SOVEREIGN LORD OUR GOD, who chose the lamp of the twelve apostles and sent them forth to proclaim the gospel of your kingdom throughout the whole world and to heal sickness and every weakness among the people, purify our lives and cleanse our hearts from all pollution and from all wickedness, that with pure heart and conscience we may be to you a sweet savor, through the grace, mercy, and love of your only begotten Son, through whom and with whom be the glory and the power to you, with your all-holy, good, and life-giving Spirit, now, henceforth, and forevermore. Amen.

THE DIVINE LITURGY OF THE HOLY APOSTLE AND EVANGELIST MARK
(BEFORE AD 200)

✚ ✚ ✚

FOR REFLECTION: Matt. 6:12-14; 26:41; Mark 14:38; Rom. 12:17; 14:10-12; 2 Cor. 5:10; 8:31; **1 Pet. 4:7**; Jude v. 3

24

Stand fast, therefore, in these things, and follow the example of the Lord. Be firm and unchangeable in the faith, loving the brotherhood, attached to one another, joined together in the truth, exhibiting the meekness of the Lord in your dealings with one another, and despising no one. When you can do good, postpone it not, because "alms deliver from death." Let all of you be subject one to another. Let your conduct be blameless among the Gentiles, that you may receive praise for your good works and that the Lord not be blasphemed through you. But woe to the one by whom the name of the Lord is blasphemed! Therefore, teach sobriety to all, and manifest it in your own conduct.

POLYCARP, *Epistle to the Philippians*, CHAP. 10

O Sovereign and Almighty God, the Father of our Lord, God, and Savior Jesus Christ, we pray and beseech you, bestow on us, O Lord, what is good and right. Whatever sin we commit, do in your goodness and mercy be pleased to pardon. Leave us not, O Lord, while we hope in you, nor lead us into temptation, but deliver us from the evil one and from his works, through the grace, mercy, and love of your only begotten Son. Through whom and with whom be glory and power to you, by your most holy, good, and life-giving Spirit, now, henceforth, and forevermore. Amen.

THE DIVINE LITURGY OF THE HOLY APOSTLE AND EVANGELIST MARK
(BEFORE AD 200)

FOR REFLECTION: Tobit 4:9-10; **12:9** (Apocrypha); Isa. 52:5; John 12:23-33; 1 Cor. 12:12-31; 1 Thess. 5:22; 2 Thess. 3:13; 1 Pet. 2:17; 4:5

25

I trust that you are well versed in the Sacred Scriptures and that nothing is hid from you. May the God and Father of our Lord Jesus Christ, and Jesus Christ himself, who is the Son of God and our everlasting High Priest, build you up in faith and truth and in all meekness, gentleness, patience, long-suffering, forbearance, and purity; and may he bestow on you a share and inheritance among his saints, on us with you, and on all that are under heaven who shall believe on our Lord Jesus Christ and in his Father who "raised him from the dead." Pray for all the saints. Pray also for kings, potentates, and princes, for those that persecute and hate you, and for the enemies of the cross, that your fruit may be manifest to all and that you may be perfect in Christ.

POLYCARP, *Epistle to the Philippians*, CHAP. 12

O MAKE YOUR CHURCH, dear Savior,
A lamp of burnish'd gold,
To bear before the nations
Thy true light as of old;
O teach your wandering pilgrims
By this, their path to trace,
Till, clouds and darkness ended,
They see you face to face. Amen.

WILLIAM WALSHAM HOW (1823-97), HYMNARY

FOR REFLECTION: Matt. 5:44; 28:7; Mark 9:10; John 15:1-11; Acts 3:15; 1 Cor. 3:9; **Gal. 1:1**, 15; 5:16-26; Eph. 2:20; Phil. 1:9-11; Col. 2:7; 1 Tim. 2:2; James 5:7

26

(This reading and the two that follow describe the martyrdom of Polycarp as recounted in a letter written by the church.)

Once the wild beasts had finished destroying the martyr Germanicus, the whole multitude, not satisfied by Germanicus's death, cried out, "Away with the Atheists; let Polycarp be sought out!" His location divulged to the authorities by tortured informants, Polycarp after praying, was brought to the stadium. The Irenarch Herod tried to convince Polycarp to save his life by sacrificing to Caesar. Polycarp refused.

As he was brought forward, the crowd became tumultuous. The proconsul asked, "Are you Polycarp?" Confessing that he was, the proconsul tried to persuade Polycarp to deny Christ. "Have respect to your old age. Swear by the genius of Caesar. Say, 'Away with the atheists [i.e., the Christians].'" But Polycarp, gazing with a stern countenance on the entire multitude, and waving his hand toward them, said, "Away with the Atheists!" Then the proconsul urged him, "Swear, and I will set you at liberty, reproach Christ." Polycarp answered, "Eighty and six years have I served him, and he never did me any injury: how then can I blaspheme my King and my Savior?"

THE *MARTYRDOM OF POLYCARP*, CHAPS. 1–9

O Lord, you are our God, who sets the captives free, who lifts up the downtrodden. Pity, relieve, and restore every Christian soul that is afflicted or wandering. Fill our hearts with joy and gladness, that at all times, having all sufficiency, we may abound to every good work in Christ Jesus our Lord. All glory, honor, adoration, and thanksgiving are due to you, the Father, Son, and Holy Ghost, now, henceforth, and forevermore. Amen.

THE DIVINE LITURGY OF THE HOLY APOSTLE AND EVANGELIST MARK
(BEFORE AD 200)

FOR REFLECTION: Matt. 24:9; Luke 9:24; Acts 6:8–7:60; Rev. 6:9-11

27

The proconsul then said to Polycarp, "I have wild beasts at hand; to these I will cast you unless you repent." But Polycarp answered, "Call them then, for we are not accustomed to repent for what is good in order to adopt what is evil; and it is well for me to be changed from what is evil to what is righteous." Again the proconsul said to him, "If you will not repent, I will cause you to be consumed by fire, seeing that you despise the wild beasts." Polycarp answered, "You threaten me with fire that burns for an hour, and after that it dies. You are ignorant of the fire of the coming judgment and of eternal punishment reserved for the ungodly. But why tarry? Bring forth what you will."

THE *MARTYRDOM OF POLYCARP*, CHAP. 11

IN DEATH'S DARK VALE *I fear no ill,*
With you, dear Lord, beside me;
Your rod and staff my comfort still,
Your cross before to guide me.

. . . .

And so, through all the length of days,
your goodness fails never;
Good Shepherd, may I sing your praise
Within your house forever! Amen.

HENRY WILLIAM BAKER (1821-77), HYMNARY

✝ ✝ ✝

FOR REFLECTION: Rom. 13:1-7; Titus 3:1; 1 Pet. 3:8–4:19; Rev. 22:5-17

28

The official in charge declared that the release of lions had ended. So it was decided that Polycarp should be burned alive. The frenzied spectators rushed to bring wood for the fire. They did not nail him but simply bound him. And he—placing his hands behind him and being bound like a distinguished ram taken out of a great flock for sacrifice and prepared to be an acceptable burnt offering to God—looked up to heaven and said, "O Lord God Almighty, the Father of your beloved and blessed Son Jesus Christ, by whom we have received knowledge of you, the God of angels and powers, of every creature, and of the whole race of the righteous who live before you, I give thanks that you have counted me worthy of this day and this hour, that I should be numbered among your martyrs, in the cup of your Christ, to the resurrection of eternal life, both of soul and body, through the incorruption imparted by the Holy Spirit. Among whom may I be accepted before you this day as a fat and acceptable sacrifice, according as you, the ever-truthful God, have foreordained, have revealed beforehand to me, and have now fulfilled. Wherefore also I praise you for all things, I bless you, I glorify you, along with the everlasting and heavenly Jesus Christ, your beloved Son, with whom to you and the Holy Spirit be glory both now and to all coming ages. Amen."

THE *MARTYRDOM OF POLYCARP*, CHAPS. 12–14

"HALLELUJAH! For the Lord our God the Almighty reigns. Let us rejoice and exult and give him the glory." Now to him who is able to bring us all into his everlasting kingdom by his grace and goodness, through his only begotten Son Jesus Christ, to him be glory, honor, power, and majesty, forever. Amen.

REV. 19:6-7, NRSV; THE *MARTYRDOM OF POLYCARP*, CHAP. 20

FOR REFLECTION: Matt. 20:22; **26:39**; **Mark 10:38**; Luke 23:27-38; Heb. 11:32–12:5

THE *SHEPHERD* OF *HERMAS*

One of the strangest pieces of early Christian literature also happened to be one of the most popular, comparable to the popularity of the later *Pilgrim's Progress* (1678). The *Shepherd* (or *Pastor*) *of Hermas* (ca. AD 100-160) is often mentioned among the Apostolic Fathers. Although many now believe the work is a novel, numerous early Christians received it as inspired Scripture. This included such prominent Christian leaders as Irenaeus, Clement of Alexandria, and Origen. The *Shepherd* was often read as Scripture in church services. Later, the Muratorian Fragment (ca. AD 180–200), the earliest-known list of New Testament books recognized by the church, rejected an early date for *Hermas*. The Muratorian Fragment instructs that while the *Shepherd* is profitable for private reading, it should not be valued as Scripture, and it should not be read in the churches. Neither the *Shepherd*'s author nor its date of composition is known with certainty. There may have been multiple authors. At any rate, many early Christians were confident the book was written by Hermas, an acquaintance of the apostle Paul mentioned in Rom. 16:14.

Hermas is the work's main character. He is shown a series of five visions, twelve commandments, and ten parables, all of which require detailed explanations by messengers sent to him. These pieces form the book's three divisions. Together, they lay out the intricate paths that lead to repentance, faith, understanding, and purity. Hermas's primary teacher is the "lady," the church, who sometimes appears as an elderly woman seated in a chair and sometimes as a virgin proceeding from the bridal chamber. The glorious and persecuted church, now being built, and the faithful discipleship in the church are unifying themes. The *Shepherd* deals with numerous church problems, including carelessness, apostasy, and the treatment of Christians who repent after they have fallen away. At the beginning of the fifth vision, a man of glorious appearance, dressed like a shepherd, is sent by an angel to guide Hermas for the rest of his life. Step-by-step, Hermas is instructed in how his shortcomings and iniquities, which are representative of shortcomings and iniquities in the church, many of which he was formerly unaware, can be cleansed. Cleansing will make it possible for Hermas to proceed along the path of holiness. He is assured that the commandments he is given can be obeyed.

The literary genre of the *Shepherd of Hermas* is Christian apocalyptic, a type of revelatory literature with a narrative framework. A revelation, or apocalypse (Greek, *apokalypsis*), is mediated by an otherworldly being to a human recipient. By using various kinds of signs and visions, an apocalypse discloses "a transcendent reality" that is "temporal" because it deals with "eschatological salvation, and spatial" because "it involves another, supernatural world."* There were many early Christian apocalypses, the biblical book of Revelation being the best known.

A contemporary reader can easily see why the *Shepherd* would have captured the attention and loyalty of early Christians. We will explore a few of the reasons.

---

*John J. Collins, "Introduction: Towards the Morphology of a Genre," in *Apocalypse: The Morphology of a Genre*, ed. John J. Collins, *Semeia* 14 (1979): 9.

29

The lady (the church) to Hermas: "Listen, and give ear to the glories of God. By his invisible strong power and great wisdom, God created the world. By his glorious counsel he surrounds his creation with beauty. By his strong word he has fixed the heavens and laid the earth's foundations on the waters. By his own wisdom and providence God created his holy church, which he has blessed. Lo! He bestows on the church the blessing he has promised, with much glory and joy, if only his people will keep the commandments they have received in great faith."

THE *SHEPHERD OF HERMAS*, BK. 1, FIRST VISION, CHAP. 3

ALL PRAISE TO OUR REDEEMING LORD,
Who joins us by his grace
And bids us, each to each restored,
Together seek his face.

He bids us build each other up;
And, gathered into one,
To our high calling's glorious hope
We hand in hand go on. Amen.

CHARLES WESLEY (1708-88), HYMNARY

FOR REFLECTION: Gen. 1:1–2:25; Neh. 9:6; Job 38:4-38; Pss. 33:6-9; 89:11-12; Isa. 45:5-13; John 1:1-14; Rev. 4:10-11; 10:6

30

The shepherd (the angel of repentance) said to me, "Be simple and guileless, and you will be as the children who know not the wickedness that ruins the life of men. First, then, speak evil of no one, nor listen with pleasure to anyone who speaks evil of another. If you listen, you will partake of the sin of him who speaks evil. For slander is evil and an unsteady demon. It never abides in peace but always remains in discord. Keep yourself from it, and you will always be at peace with all. Put on a holiness in which there is no wicked cause of offence, but all deeds that are even tempered and joyful. Practice goodness; and from the rewards of your labors, which God gives you, give to all the needy in simplicity, not hesitating as to whom you are to give or not give. Give to all, for God wishes his gifts to be shared among all. Those who receive will render an account to God why and for what reason they have received. The afflicted who receive will not be condemned, but those who receive on false pretenses will suffer punishment. The person who ministers in simplicity will live to God."

THE *SHEPHERD OF HERMAS*, BK. 2, COMMANDMENT 2

WE PRAY AND BESEECH THEE, O lover of all people, O good Lord, remember in your good mercy your church throughout the world and all your people. Grant to the hearts of us all the peace of heaven, but grant us also the peace of this life. May we be yours, O Lord, for we know no other God but you and name no other name but yours. Give us life, and let no deadly sin prevail against us, or against your people. For you are the One who blesses and sanctifies all things. To you we ascribe honor, glory, and thanksgiving. Amen.

THE DIVINE LITURGY OF THE HOLY APOSTLE AND EVANGELIST MARK
(BEFORE AD 200)

FOR REFLECTION: Pss. 37:3-8; 40:1-10; Prov. 12:1-7, 26-28; 22:1; Mic. 6:8; Matt. 25:34-40; 1 John 3:17-18

31

The shepherd said to me, "Love the truth, and let nothing but truth proceed from your mouth, that the spirit that God has placed in your flesh may be found truthful before all people; and the Lord, who dwells in you, will be glorified because he is truthful in every word, and in him there is no falsehood. They therefore who lie deny the Lord and rob him, not giving back to him the deposit that they have received. For they received from him a spirit free of falsehood. If they give back to God this spirit as being untruthful, they will pollute the commandments of the Lord and become robbers."

THE *SHEPHERD OF HERMAS*, BK. 2, COMMANDMENT 3

O SOVEREIGN AND ALMIGHTY LORD, look down from heaven on your church, on all your people, and on all your flock. Save us all, your unworthy servants, the sheep of your fold. Give us your peace, your help, and your love, and send to us the gift of your Holy Spirit, that with a pure heart and a good conscience we may salute one another with a holy kiss, without hypocrisy, and with no hostile purpose. Make us guileless and pure in one spirit, in the bond of peace and love, one body and one spirit, in one faith, even as we have been called in one hope of our calling, that we may all meet in the divine and boundless love, in Christ Jesus our Lord, with whom you are blessed. For all glory, honor, adoration, and thanks are due to you, the Father, Son, and Holy Spirit, now, henceforth, and forevermore. Amen.

THE DIVINE LITURGY OF THE HOLY APOSTLE AND EVANGELIST MARK
(BEFORE AD 200)

FOR REFLECTION: 1 Sam. 12:24; 2 Kings 20:1-5; Pss. 25:4-14; 86:1-17; John 1:15-18; 4:24; 14:6; **Eph. 4:25, 29**; 1 John 3:19-21; 4:6

32

"Hear now," said the shepherd, "how wicked is the action of anger, and in what way it overthrows the servants of God and turns them away from righteousness. But it does not act on those who are full of faith, nor does it turn them away from righteousness, for the power of the Lord is in them. Anger turns away the thoughtless and doubting. For as soon as it sees such people, it throws itself into their hearts, and for nothing at all the person becomes embittered on account of occurrences in life, maybe because of food, some superfluous word that has been spoken, some friend, some gift or debt, or some such senseless affair. For all these things are foolish and empty and unprofitable to the servants of God. But patience is great, mighty, strong, and calm in the midst of great increase, joyful, rejoicing, free from care, glorifying God at all times, having no bitterness in her, and abiding in the Lord continually, meek and quiet. Depart from anger—that most wicked spirit—and you will be found in company with the purity the Lord loves."

THE *SHEPHERD OF HERMAS*, BK. 2, COMMANDMENT 5

DELIVER THE CAPTIVE; rescue the distressed; feed the hungry; comfort the fainthearted; convert the erring; enlighten the darkened; raise the fallen; confirm the wavering; heal the sick; and guide them all, good Lord, into the way of salvation and into your sacred fold. Deliver us from our iniquities; protect and defend us at all times. All glory, honor, adoration, and thanks are due to you, the Father, Son, and Holy Spirit, now, henceforth, and forevermore. Amen.

THE DIVINE LITURGY OF THE HOLY APOSTLE AND EVANGELIST MARK
(BEFORE AD 200)

FOR REFLECTION: Matt. 5:22; Gal. 5:19-26; Eph. 4:26-27; Col. 3:8; Titus 1:7; James 3:11

THE *EPISTLE TO DIOGNETUS* [*MATHETES*]

The *Epistle to Diognetus* (ca. AD 130) was written by an anonymous Christian who gave himself the name Mathetes, or "Disciple" (of the Apostles). Unlike writings of the Apostolic Fathers that speak to other Christians, the *Epistle to Diognetus* is written to a learned Greco-Roman pagan. It is actually classed as an apology for (a defense of) the Christian faith. But the work is usually listed among the Apostolic Fathers, and so we will leave it here.

We know very little about Mathetes, including where or when he wrote his letter. He might have been a pupil of the apostle Paul or one of Paul's associates. The epistle is important because it breathes the spirit of the apostle Paul and illustrates how Christians communicated with their pagan neighbors when attempting to lead them to Christian conversion. In simple language, the letter admirably defends the Christian way against Greco-Roman paganism. It surgically dissects pagan religion, something the early Christian writers did relentlessly. The epistle has been called a "gem of purest ray."*

Diognetus, the letter's intended recipient, might have been the tutor of Emperor Marcus Aurelius (r. AD 161-80), who was also a Stoic philosopher. Whoever the intended recipient, he was interested in learning about how Christians worship God and how they live.

---

*A. Cleveland Coxe, "Introductory Note to the Epistle of Mathetes to Diognetus," in *The Apostolic Fathers, Justin Martyr, Irenaeus*, vol. 1, *Ante-Nicene Fathers* (1885; repr., Peabody, MA: Hendrickson Publishers, 1994), 23.

33

(The writer of the epistle discusses the vanity of idols.)

Is not one of your gods a stone similar to that on which we walk? Is not a second made of brass, in no way superior to those vessels that are crafted for ordinary use? Is not a third made of wood, and that already rotting? Is not a fourth silver, which needs someone to guard it against theft? Is not a fifth iron, now being consumed by rust? Is not a sixth god simple earthenware, in no sense more valuable than that which is formed for the humblest of purposes? Are not all these of corruptible matter? Did not the sculptor fashion one of them, the brazier a second, the silversmith a third, and the potter a fourth? Are not all your gods deaf? Are they not blind? Are they not dead? Are they not void of feeling? Are they not incapable of movement? These things you call gods; these you serve; these you worship; and in the process you have become just like them.

THE *EPISTLE TO DIOGNETUS*, CHAP. 2

PRAISE TO THE LIVING GOD!
All praised be his name,
Who was, and is, and is to be,
For aye the same.
The one eternal God
Ere aught that now appears:
The first, the last, beyond all thought
His timeless years. Amen.
DANIEL BEN JUDAH (CA. AD 1400), TRANS. MAX LANDSBERG (1845–1928),
HYMNARY

FOR REFLECTION: Ps. 16:4; Isa. 42:17; Act 17:16-31; 1 Cor. 10:13-22; 1 John 5:21

34

The Conduct of Christians: Christians are distinguished from other people neither by country nor by language nor by the customs they observe. For they neither inhabit cities of their own nor employ a peculiar form of speech nor lead a life that is marked out by any peculiarity. Their course of conduct was not devised by speculation or deliberation practiced by inquisitive men. Nor do Christians, like some, proclaim themselves the advocates of merely human doctrines. Instead, inhabiting Greek as well as barbarian cities, as the lot of each has determined, and following the customs of the locals in respect to clothing, food, and the rest of their ordinary conduct, they display their wonderful and confessedly striking way of life. They dwell in their own countries, but simply as sojourners. As citizens, they share in all things with others, and yet they endure all things as if foreigners. Every foreign land is to them as their native country, and every land of their birth as a land of strangers.

THE *EPISTLE TO DIOGNETUS*, CHAP. 5

O LORD GOD, SOVEREIGN AND ALMIGHTY FATHER, truly it is meet and right, holy and becoming, and good for our souls to praise, bless, and thank you; to make open confession to you by day and night with voice, lips, and heart without ceasing. Truly heaven and earth are full of your glory, through the manifestation of our Lord and God and Savior Jesus Christ. Sanctify us as living sacrifices, holy and acceptable to you, which is our spiritual worship, through the ministration of your all-holy Spirit. Amen.

THE DIVINE LITURGY OF THE HOLY APOSTLE AND EVANGELIST MARK
(BEFORE AD 200)

FOR REFLECTION: Rom. 12:3-21; 13:1-14; James 3:17-18; 1 Pet. 4:7-19; Jude vv. 17-25

35

The Conduct of Christians (continued): Christians marry, as do others; they beget children, but they do not destroy their offspring. They have a common table but not a common bed. They are in the flesh, but they do not live after the flesh. They pass their days on earth, but they are citizens of heaven. They obey prescribed laws, and at the same time their lives surpass those laws. They love all people and are persecuted by all. They are unknown and yet condemned; they are put to death and are yet restored to life. They are poor, yet make many rich; they are in need of all things, and yet they abound; they are dishonored, and yet in their very dishonor they are glorified. They are evil spoken of and yet are justified; they are reviled, and yet they bless; they are insulted, and they repay the insult with honor; they do good and yet are punished as evildoers. When punished, they rejoice as if quickened into life; they are assailed by the Jews as foreigners and are persecuted by the Greeks; yet those who hate them are unable to assign any reason for their hatred.

THE *EPISTLE TO DIOGNETUS*, CHAP. 5

HAVE MERCY ON US, O LORD, and strengthen us by your divine power. Take away from us the sinful and wicked influence of carnal desire. Let your light shine into our hearts and dispel the surrounding darkness of sin. Unite us to the all-blessed assembly, the church; for through you and with you, all praise, honor, power, adoration, and thanksgiving are due, with the Father and the Holy Spirit, now and forevermore. Amen.

THE DIVINE LITURGY OF THE HOLY APOSTLE AND EVANGELIST MARK
(BEFORE AD 200)

FOR REFLECTION: Matt. 10:16-28; Luke 21:12-19; 1 Cor. 4:1-14; Eph. 4:11–6:24; 1 Pet. 3:1-18

36

The Manifestation of Christ: No mere earthly invention was delivered to Christians, nor did they receive a mere human system of opinion. Neither has a dispensation of mere human mysteries been committed to them. Truly God himself, who is almighty, the Creator of all things and invisible, has sent from heaven and placed among humans the One who is truth, the holy and incomprehensible Word. God has firmly established the Word in their hearts. He did not send to humankind a mere human servant, angel, or ruler or any among those who have power over earthly things. He sent the very Creator and Fashioner of all things. By him, the heavens were made. By him, God enclosed the sea within its proper limits. His ordinances all the stars faithfully observe. From him the sun has received the span of its daily course. Him the moon obeys, being commanded to shine in the night, and the stars obey him, by whom they were arranged and placed in their proper limits. To him all things are subject—the heavens and the things that are therein, the earth and the things that are therein, the sea and the things that are therein, the things in the heights, the things in the depths, and all that lies between.

THE *EPISTLE TO DIOGNETUS*, CHAP. 7

O Lord, be merciful to us and pity us, for you are our Helper in all circumstances, O Lord of all. Enlighten the movements of our meditations to hear and understand your life-giving and divine commands; and grant to us through your grace and mercy to gather from them the assurance of your love, hope, and salvation suitable to soul and body. We shall sing to you everlasting glory without ceasing and always, O Lord of all. Amen.

ADAEUS AND MARIS, THE LITURGY OF THE BLESSED APOSTLES (CA. AD 150)

FOR REFLECTION: John 1:1-14; 17:1-26; Acts 2:14-49; Heb. 1:1-14; 1 John 2:22-24; 4:1-3

37

The Manifestation of Christ (continued): This Messenger God sent to Christians. Was it then, as one might expect, for the purpose of exercising tyranny or of inspiring fear and terror? By no means, but in a spirit of mercy and meekness he came. As a king sends his son, who is also a king, so God sent Christ; as God, he sent him; as to men, he sent him; as a Savior, he sent him, and as seeking to persuade, not to compel us; for such violence has no place in the character of God. As calling us, the Father sent him, not as vengefully pursuing us; as loving us, he sent him, not as condemning us. One day he will send Christ to judge us, and who shall endure his appearing? Do you not see Christians exposed to wild beasts that they may be persuaded to deny the Lord, and yet they are not overcome? Do you not see that the more of them are punished, the greater becomes their number? This does not seem to be the work of man. This is the work of God.

THE *EPISTLE TO DIOGNETUS*, CHAP. 7

LET ALL MORTAL FLESH KEEP SILENCE,
  And with fear and trembling stand;
Ponder nothing earthly minded,
  For with blessing in his hand,
Christ our God to earth descendeth,
  Our full homage to demand. Amen.

A CHERUBIC HYMN FOR THE OFFERTORY, ADAPTED FROM THE DIVINE
LITURGY OF JAMES THE HOLY APOSTLE (CA. AD 150–200),
TRANS. GERARD MOULTRIE (1829-85), HYMNARY

FOR REFLECTION: Rom. 3:20-28; 1 Cor. 1:17-31; Eph. 1:3-23; Phil. 2:1-11

38

When punishment and death were threatening humans because of our sins, and when the time came that God had appointed for manifesting his kindness and power, he acted with exceeding mercy toward us. He did not act in hatred, nor did he cast us away, nor did he remember our iniquity against us. Rather, he showed great long-suffering and was patient with us. God himself took on himself the burden of our iniquities. He gave his own Son as a ransom for us, the Holy One for the transgressors, the Blameless One for the wicked, the Righteous One for the unrighteous, the Incorruptible One for the corruptible, and the Immortal One for those who are mortal. For what other deed was capable of covering our sins than Christ's righteousness? By what other was it possible that we, the wicked and ungodly, could be reconciled than by the only Son of God?

THE *EPISTLE TO DIOGNETUS*, CHAP. 9

AT HIS FEET THE SIX-WINGED SERAPH;
Cherubim with sleepless eye,
Veil their faces to the presence,
As with ceaseless voice they cry,
"Alleluia, alleluia,
Alleluia, Lord most high!" Amen.

A CHERUBIC HYMN FOR THE OFFERTORY, ADAPTED FROM
THE DIVINE LITURGY OF JAMES THE HOLY APOSTLE (CA. AD 150–200),
TRANS. GERARD MOULTRIE (1829-85), HYMNARY

FOR REFLECTION: Isa. 53:1-12; John 3:14-21; 10:7-18; Heb. 2:1-10

39

O sweet exchange! O unsearchable operation! O benefits sur-
passing all expectation! That the wickedness of many should
be hid in a single Righteous One, and that the righteousness
of One should justify many transgressors! Having therefore
convinced us in the former time that our nature was unable to
attain to life, and having now revealed the Savior who is able
to save even those things that it was beforehand impossible
to save, he led us to trust in his kindness, to esteem him our
Nourisher, Father, Teacher, Counselor, Healer, our Wisdom,
Light, Honor, Glory, Power, and Life, so that we should not be
anxious about clothing and food.

THE *EPISTLE TO DIOGNETUS*, CHAP. 9

LORD JESUS CHRIST, *you stretched out your arms of love on the hard wood of the
cross that everyone might come within the reach of your saving embrace: So clothe
us in your Spirit that we, reaching forth our hands in love, may bring those who
do not know you to the knowledge and love of you; for the honor of your name.
Amen.*

"A COLLECT FOR GUIDANCE," DAILY MORNING PRAYER: RITE TWO, IN BCP

FOR REFLECTION: Rom. 5:1-21; Col. 2:6-15; 3:1-17; Heb. 10:12-23;
1 Pet. 1:3-25

40

It is not by ruling over our neighbors, seeking to lord it over the weak, becoming rich, or acting violently toward those who are inferior that happiness is found. Nor can anyone by these things become an imitator of God. Such things do not at all constitute God's majesty. On the contrary, he who takes on himself the burden of his neighbor; he who, in whatsoever respect he may be superior, is ready to provide for another who is deficient; he who, whatsoever things he has received from God, by distributing them to the needy, becomes like God to those who receive the gifts—that person is an imitator of God.

THE EPISTLE TO DIOGNETUS, CHAP. 10

LEAD US, HEAVENLY FATHER, lead us
  O'er the world's tempestuous sea;
Guard us, guide us, keep us, feed us,
  For we have no help but thee:
Yet possessing
Every blessing,
  If our God our Father be. Amen.

JAMES EDMESTON (1791–1867), HYMNARY

✦ ✦ ✦

FOR REFLECTION: Matt. 5:1-12; Rom. 12:6-21; 1 Cor. 13:1-13; Phil. 2:1-11; 1 Tim. 6:17-21; James 1:22-27

41

If you become an imitator of God, then you will see, while still on earth, that God in the heavens rules over all; then you will begin to speak the mysteries of God; then you will both love and admire those who suffer punishment because they will not deny God; then you will condemn the deceit and error of the world. You will know what it is to live in heaven when you despise what the world dismisses as deadly, when you fear what is truly deadly. Then you will esteem those who for righteousness' sake endure the persecution that lasts but a moment, and will count them as happy.

THE *EPISTLE TO DIOGNETUS*, CHAP. 10

O GOD, the King eternal, who divides the day from the night and turns the shadow of death into the morning: Drive far from us all wrong desires, incline our hearts to keep your law, and guide our feet into the way of peace; that, having done your will with cheerfulness during the day, we may, when night comes, rejoice to give you thanks; through Jesus Christ our Lord. Amen.

"A COLLECT FOR THE RENEWAL OF LIFE," DAILY MORNING PRAYER: RITE TWO, IN BCP

FOR REFLECTION: 2 Cor. 4:11-18; Heb. 12:1-8; 1 Pet. 3:8–4:19; Rev. 21:1-8; 22:6-14

THE GREEK APOLOGISTS

The next fathers to teach us are the Greek apologists. They began to appear toward the middle of the second century. The word "apologist" comes from a Greek word, *apologia,* which means "to give an answer for or a defense of" something one believes to be true. The apologists were the first to explain the Christian faith to classical culture, to argue for its superiority, and to defend against pagan (and sometimes Jewish) attacks. In the process, they exposed the errors of pagan religion and discussed the shortcomings of the philosophers. Some of them noted favorable similarities between certain Christian beliefs and certain ideas of the philosophers. Notable among the apologists was their acquaintance with the bewildering array of pagan deities and their origins.

Although the apologists often addressed their defenses to emperors, the defenses were intended for wider audiences. Often a Christian apologist would make use of a "bridge" or tenet common to both parties and employ it to explain his or her position. The apostle Paul did this when speaking to the Stoics and Epicureans in Athens (Acts 17:16-31). In the thirteenth century Thomas Aquinas (ca. 1225-74) would use the philosopher Aristotle as a middle ground to begin addressing the gospel to the Muslims. An apologist using this strategy would grant that their audience possessed beforehand a measure of correct understanding, such as religious insights arrived at by Plato, Aristotle, or the Stoics, that prepared the way for the perfect understanding the apologist offered. The aim was not only to defend but also to convince. Not all apologists used this approach. Some saw only bitter conflict between Greco-Roman culture and the Christian faith. Others believed that some Greek philosophers had partially seen the truth and that the Logos had even aided those philosophers.

One danger associated with apologetics is that efforts to establish a "bridge" can result in compromising or misrepresenting something essential to the apologist's own position. Whatever the apologists' tactics, in their attempts to explain the Christian faith they found it necessary to spell out Christian claims in systematic ways that had not previously been required. Their sincere efforts sometimes led them to say things less precisely than other Christian thinkers and the later church councils would do. In sum, the apologists' service to the early church was admirable and essential, for not only did they explain the Christian faith, but they also dissected polytheism and showed the folly of continuing its practice. There is a long list of Greek apologists, some of whose writings are lost.

ARISTIDES

Around the year AD 125 a Christian identified as Aristides the Philosopher of Athens addressed an apology to the "venerable and merciful" Emperor Hadrian (r. AD 117-38) when the emperor was visiting Athens. His apology is said to have been the inspiration for the works of Justin Martyr. Aristides says there are four classes of humans: barbarians, Greeks, Jews, and Christians. Apparently the Egyptians, whom he judged to be "more base and stupid than every people" (*Apology,* chap. 12), didn't even count. Each class has its characteristic religion, only one of which, namely, the Christians, faithfully expresses the one true God.

According to Aristides, the barbarians went astray because they worshipped created elements instead of the Creator. They made images and placed them in shrines. The Greeks, though more cultured, went further astray than the barbarians by creating fictitious male and female gods. Some were adulterers, some murderers, some envious, some wrathful, some thieves and robbers, some crippled, some sorcerers, while others even killed their parents. Then, to make matters worse, the Greeks were encouraged to imitate their gods. Aristides thought the Jews, by worshipping one God who is the Creator of heaven and earth, approached the truth more correctly than other peoples. But they fell into idolatry. They rendered service more to angels and their own laws than to God. By contrast, Christians traced the beginning of their religion to Jesus the Messiah, who is the Son of God Most High.

42

Christians, O King, know and trust in God, the Creator of heaven and earth, in whom and from whom are all things, and for whom there is no other god or companion. From him, Christians have received commandments that are engraved on their minds. They observe these commandments in hope and expectation of the world to come. Because of this, they commit neither adultery nor fornication, nor do they bear false witness, nor do they embezzle what they hold in pledge, nor do they covet what is not theirs. They honor father and mother and show kindness to those near to them. When they must judge, they judge uprightly. They do not worship idols made in the image of humans; and what they would not want others to do to them, they don't do to others.

THE *APOLOGY* OF ARISTIDES THE PHILOSOPHER OF ATHENS, CHAP. 15

HEAVENLY FATHER, in you we live and move and have our being: We humbly pray you so to guide and govern us by your Holy Spirit, that in all the cares and occupations of our life we may not forget you, but may remember that we are ever walking in your sight; through Jesus Christ our Lord. Amen.

"A COLLECT FOR GUIDANCE," DAILY MORNING PRAYER: RITE TWO, IN BCP

FOR REFLECTION: Luke 6:17-49; 1 Thess. 5:1-15; Titus 2:11–3:8; Heb. 13:20-21

43

Christians comfort their oppressors and make them their friends; they do good to their enemies. Their young unmarried women, O King, are pure as virgins. Their daughters are modest. Their men keep themselves from every unlawful union and from all uncleanness, in the hope of a recompense to come in the other world. Further, if one or other of them have bondmen and bondwomen or children, through love toward them they persuade them to become Christians, and when they have done so, they call them brethren without distinction.

THE *APOLOGY* OF ARISTIDES THE PHILOSOPHER OF ATHENS, CHAP. 15

THE KING OF LOVE my Shepherd is,
   Whose goodness faileth never.
I nothing lack if I am his,
   And he is mine forever.

Where streams of living water flow
   My ransomed soul he leadeth;
And where the verdant pastures grow,
   With food celestial feedeth.

   . . . .

And so, through all the length of days,
   Your goodness faileth never;
Good Shepherd, may I sing your praise
   Within your house forever. Amen.

HENRY WILLIAMS BAKER (1821-77), HYMNARY

✚ ✚ ✚

FOR REFLECTION: Exod. 20:1-17; Ps. 19:1-3; Jer. 4:1-4; 1 Cor. 5:8–6:20; 1 John 5:11-21

44

Christians do not worship strange gods, and they go their way with all modesty and cheerfulness. Falsehood is not found among them; and they love one another. From widows they do not turn away their respect; and they deliver the orphan from the one who treats him cruelly. He who has, gives to him who has not, without boasting. When Christians see a stranger, they take him into their homes and rejoice over him as a very brother; for they do not call one another "brethren" after the flesh, but "brethren" after the Spirit, and in God. And whenever one of their poor passes from the world, each one of them, according to his ability, gives heed to him and carefully sees to his burial. If they hear that one of their number is imprisoned or afflicted on account of the name of their Messiah, all of them anxiously minister to his necessity, and if it is possible to redeem him, they set him free. If there is among them any that are poor and needy, and if they do not have enough food, the Christians will fast two or three days to supply sufficient food.

THE *APOLOGY* OF ARISTIDES THE PHILOSOPHER OF ATHENS, CHAP. 15

SEARCH OUT OUR HEARTS AND MAKE US TRUE;
Help us to give to all their due.
From love of pleasure, lust of gold,
From sins which make the heart grow cold,
Wean us and train us with thy rod;
Teach us to know our faults, O God. Amen.

WILLIAM B. CARPENTER (1841–1918), HYMNARY

FOR REFLECTION: Pss. 96:5; 115:4-8; 135:15-18; Isa. 40:18-26; Rom. 14:1-19; 1 Cor. 12:2

45

Christians carefully observe the precepts of their Messiah, living justly and soberly as the Lord their God commands. Every morning and every hour they give thanks and praise to God for his loving-kindnesses toward them. For their food and drink they offer thanksgiving. If any righteous person among them passes from the world, they rejoice and offer thanks to God; and they escort his body as if he were setting out from one place to another nearby. When a child has been born to one of them, they give thanks to God; and if the child happens to die in childhood, they give thanks to God the more, as for one who has passed through the world without sin. And further, if they see that any one of them dies in his ungodliness or in his sins, for him they grieve bitterly and sorrow as for one who goes to meet his doom.

THE *APOLOGY* OF ARISTIDES THE PHILOSOPHER OF ATHENS, CHAP. 15

O LORD, OUR HEAVENLY FATHER, almighty and everlasting God, who hast safely brought us to the beginning of this day: Defend us in the same with your mighty power; and grant that this day we fall into no sin, neither run into any kind of danger; but that we, being ordered by your governance, may do always what is righteous in your sight; through Jesus Christ our Lord. Amen.

"A COLLECT FOR GRACE," DAILY MORNING PRAYER: RITE ONE, IN BCP

FOR REFLECTION: Pss. 40:1-10; 98:1-9; 118:1-4; Eph. 5:17-21; Phil. 3:8-16; Heb. 13:15

46

Such, O King, is the commandment by which the Christians live, and such is their conduct of life. As people who know God, they make petitions that are fitting for God to grant and for them to receive. Such petitions they make their whole lifetime. And because they know the loving-kindnesses of God, behold, for them the beautiful things in the world come into view. And truly, they found the truth when they searched for it; they alone come near to knowledge of the truth. They do not boast to the multitudes about the kind deeds they do but are careful that no one should notice them; and they conceal their giving just as he who finds a treasure and conceals it.

THE *APOLOGY* OF ARISTIDES THE PHILOSOPHER OF ATHENS, CHAP. 16

O GOD, the King eternal, whose light divides the day from the night and turns the shadow of death into the morning: Drive far from us all wrong desires, incline our hearts to keep your law, and guide our feet into the way of peace; that, having done your will with cheerfulness during the day, we may, when night comes, rejoice to give you thanks; through Jesus Christ our Lord. Amen.

"A COLLECT FOR THE RENEWAL OF LIFE," DAILY MORNING PRAYER: RITE TWO, IN BCP

FOR REFLECTION: Ps. 117:1-2; Isa. 54:1-11; Matt. 6:1-15; 25:34-36; John 14:5-14

47

Christians strive to be righteous as persons who expect to behold their Messiah, and to receive from him with great glory the promises he has made. As for their words and their precepts, O King, and how they glorify God in their worship, and their hope of being recompensed in another world according to how they have lived, you can learn about all these things in their writings. Great indeed and wonderful is their doctrine for the person who will search into it and reflect on it. And truly, Christians are a new people; there is a divine presence in the midst of them.

THE *APOLOGY* OF ARISTIDES THE PHILOSOPHER OF ATHENS, CHAP. 16

O SOVEREIGN LORD CHRIST JESUS, the coeternal Word of the eternal Father, who was made in all things as we are, but without sin, for the salvation of our race; who has sent forth your holy disciples and apostles to proclaim and teach the gospel of your kingdom and to heal all disease, all sickness among your people, be pleased now, O Lord, to send forth your light and your truth. Enlighten the eyes of our minds, that we may understand your divine oracles. Fit us to become hearers, and not only hearers but also doers of your word, that we, becoming fruitful and yielding good fruit from thirty to a hundredfold, may be deemed worthy of the kingdom of heaven. Amen.

THE DIVINE LITURGY OF THE HOLY APOSTLE AND EVANGELIST MARK
(BEFORE AD 200)

FOR REFLECTION: Matt. 25:34-46; Luke 6:22-23, 25; 2 Cor. 5:14-21; 1 Pet. 3:9-12; Rev. 1:17-20; 3:21-22

JUSTIN MARTYR

The most important second-century Greek apologist was a philosopher who had been a student of numerous philosophical systems, including those of Socrates and Plato, before becoming a Christian. After his conversion, he continued to dress in the philosopher's garb because he believed that in Christianity he had finally found the true philosophy; in Christianity all philosophy is fulfilled. We know him as Justin Martyr (ca. AD 100-ca. 165), a Gentile born in Samaria near Jacob's well. He was well educated and had traveled extensively. Justin had the intellectual gifts and training needed to present the gospel of Jesus the Galilean to reflective Greco-Roman minds. He became a "star" in the West that led enquirers to Bethlehem's stable. Justin believed that unlike any of the philosophers, Jesus Christ fulfilled the expectations of those from every nation who waited for the good things of God. Regardless of human rank, the gospel of Christ addresses everyone. Wise people will abandon the old failed philosophies and the old pagan deities and will love only the truth as found in Jesus.

Justin tells those who persecute Christians just because of their name that to be fair they must first examine the true meaning of the term, a service Justin provides. Once this happens, opponents will see the wrong involved in accusing and persecuting Christians. His opponents did not listen; Justin was martyred in Rome around AD 165, during the reign of Marcus Aurelius (AD 161-80).

There are three works by Justin whose authorship is certain. A *First Apology* is addressed to Emperor Antoninus Pius (r. AD 138-61), his son Verissimus, Lucius the Philosopher, the Senate, and all Romans. A *Second Apology* is addressed to the Roman Senate. The *Dialogue with Trypho* was written in Ephesus (ca. AD 150) and is a purported dialogue with the most celebrated Jew of the day. There are other works, but their authorship is not certain.

48

(Justin has charged that even some of the philosophers were atheists, that the poets lampoon the immorality of Jupiter, and that the Romans grant approval and prizes to the poets who ridicule the gods.)

How hypocritical that the Christians would be persecuted as atheists. You call us atheists because we cannot point to a shrine or temple for our God. We confess that we are atheists, so far as your kind of gods are concerned, but not with respect to the most true God. He is the Father of righteousness and temperance and the other virtues. He is free from all impurity. But both he and the Son who came forth from him and taught us these things, and the prophetic Spirit, we worship and adore. We know them in reason and truth and teach this truth to all who wish to learn, even as we have been taught.

THE *FIRST APOLOGY* OF JUSTIN MARTYR, CHAPS. 5–6, 9–10

BREATHE ON ME, BREATH OF GOD,
Fill me with life anew,
That I may love what thou dost love,
And do what thou wouldst do.

Breathe on me, Breath of God,
Until my heart is pure,
Until with thee I will thy will,
To do and to endure.

Breathe on me, Breath of God,
Till I am wholly thine,
Till all this earthly part of me
Glows with thy fire divine. Amen.

EDWIN HATCH (1835-89), HYMNARY

FOR REFLECTION: Ps. 89:1-18; Jer. 9:23-25; Acts 17:22-31; Rom. 1:18-26; 12:1-2; Rev. 14:6-7

49

When we are examined prior to torture, imprisonment, or martyrdom, it is within our power to deny that we are Christians. But we do not live by telling lies. Prompted by a desire for the eternal and pure life, we seek the abode that is with God, the Father and Creator of all. We hasten to confess our faith. We are persuaded that those who have by their works shown to God that they followed him, and longed to abide with him where there is no sin to cause disturbance, will possess these things. If anyone says that this is incredible or impossible, this "error" of ours is one that concerns us only, and no other person, so long as you cannot convict us of doing wrong.

THE *FIRST APOLOGY* OF JUSTIN MARTYR, CHAP. 8

O GOD,
I bind to myself today
    The strong name of the Trinity
By invocation of the same,
    The Three in One, and One in Three.

I bind to myself today
    The power of God to hold and lead,
His eye to watch, his might to stay,
    His ear to harken to my need,
The wisdom of my God to teach,
    His hand to guide, his shield to ward,
The Word of God to give me speech,
    His heavenly host to be my guard. Amen.

PATRICK (CA. AD 387–CA. 463), TRANS. CECIL F. ALEXANDER (1889),
HYMNARY

FOR REFLECTION: Matt. 25:14-23; Luke 16:10-12; 2 Cor. 4:1–5:11; Rev. 2:10

50

Christians do not honor with sacrifices and garlands of flowers the deities humans have created and placed in shrines. We know they are lifeless, dead, and do not have the form of God, who has no physical form. You already know that craftsmen carve, cut, and hammer to fashion physical matter into gods, often out of vessels of dishonor. By merely changing the shape and making the image as required, the craftsmen create a god. We consider this not only senseless but also insulting to God; he who has inexpressible glory and form has his name associated with corruptible things that require constant maintenance. You very well know that the creators of these gods are themselves intemperate and practice every kind of vice. You well know that even their own girls who work along with them are corrupt. What folly, that immoral men should create the gods you worship, and that you should make these men the guardians of your temples! Do you not realize how foolish it is to say that men can be guardians of gods?

THE *FIRST APOLOGY* OF JUSTIN MARTYR, CHAP. 9

GLORY BE TO GOD ON HIGH,
God in whom we live and die,
God, who guides us by his love,
Takes us to his throne above!
Angels that surround his throne
Sing the wonders he hath done,
Shout, while we on earth reply,
Glory be to God on high! Amen.

A *COLLECTION OF HYMNS FOR THE USE OF THE PEOPLE CALLED METHODISTS* (1889), HYMN 53

FOR REFLECTION: Exod. 20:3-6; Deut. 27:15; Isa. 44:9-20; Jer. 10:3; 1 Cor. 10:19-23

51

(Justin shows the contrast between Christian and pagan worship.)

Christians have been taught that God does not need the material offerings humans can give, seeing that he himself is the provider of all things. And we have been taught and are convinced that God accepts those who imitate the excellences that reside in him—temperance, justice, and love for all people. And we have been taught that in the beginning God did of his goodness, for humanity's sake, create all things. If by their deeds Christians prove themselves faithful to God's purpose, they will reign in company with him, being delivered from corruption and suffering. As in the beginning, God created us out of nothing that preexisted; in like manner, those who choose what is pleasing to him will be given incorruption and fellowship with him. For the coming into being at first was not in our own power, and so that we may follow those things that please him, choosing them by way of the rational faculties with which he has endowed us, he both persuades us and leads us to faith.

THE *FIRST APOLOGY* OF JUSTIN MARTYR, CHAP. 10

AT THE NAME OF JESUS
Every knee shall bow,
Every tongue confess him
King of glory now;
'Tis the Father's pleasure
We should call him Lord,
Who from the beginning
Was the mighty Word. Amen.

CAROLINE MARIA NOEL (1817-77), HYMNARY

FOR REFLECTION: 1 Chron. 16:23-36; Neh. 9:4-15; Job 9:8-9; 38:4-38; Isa. 45:7-18

52

What sober-minded person, then, will not acknowledge that we are not atheists? We worship the Creator of the universe. We declare as we have been taught that God has no need for streams of blood, libations, and incense. Through prayer and thanksgiving we praise him for all things he has given. We have been taught that the honor worthy of God is not to consume by altar fires what he has given but to use it for ourselves and for those in need. With gratitude we offer our thanks to God. Through prayers and hymns we thank him for our creation, for health, for the qualities of various kinds of things, and for the changing seasons. In faith we place before him petitions for our resurrection to incorruption. Our teacher of all these things is Jesus Christ. He was born for this purpose and was crucified under Pontius Pilate in the times of Tiberius Caesar. We justifiably worship him, having learned that he is the Son of the true God. Our accusers say that our madness consists in calling a crucified man the Son of the unchangeable and eternal God, the Creator of all.

THE *FIRST APOLOGY* OF JUSTIN MARTYR, CHAP. 13

LOVE DIVINE! WHAT HAST THOU DONE!
The immortal God hath died for me!
The Fathers coeternal Son
Bore all my sins upon the tree;
The immortal God for me hath died!
My Lord, my Love is crucified. Amen.

A COLLECTION OF HYMNS FOR THE USE OF THE PEOPLE CALLED METHODISTS (1889),
HYMN 28

✜ ✜ ✜

FOR REFLECTION: Ezra 9:5-8; Pss. 76:11; 96:8; Mark 8:27-33; 9:2-9; 1 Cor. 1:17-31; Rev. 14:7; 19:10

53

(Justin discusses Christian baptism, also known as illumination.)

All who are persuaded and believe that what we teach is true, and want to live accordingly, are instructed to pray and to entreat God with fasting for the remission of their past sins. We pray and fast with them. Then in the name of God the Father and Lord of the universe, and of our Savior Jesus Christ, and of the Holy Spirit, they receive the washing with water. Christ taught us: "Unless you are born again, you shall not enter the kingdom of heaven." In order that we may become the children of choice and knowledge and may obtain in baptism the remission of sins formerly committed, there is pronounced over him who chooses to be born again and has repented of his sins the name of God the Father and Lord of the universe. This washing is called illumination, because the baptized are illuminated in their understanding. And in the name of Jesus Christ, who was crucified under Pontius Pilate, and in the name of the Holy Spirit, who through the prophets foretold all things about Jesus, he who is illuminated is washed.

THE *FIRST APOLOGY* OF JUSTIN MARTYR, CHAP. 61

CHRIST BE WITH ME, *Christ within me,*
Christ in quiet, Christ in danger,
Christ in hearts of all that love me,
Christ in mouth of friend and stranger. Amen.
PATRICK (CA. AD 387–CA. 463), TRANS. CECIL F. ALEXANDER (1889),
HYMNARY

FOR REFLECTION: John 3:1-13; Acts 9:18; 10:1-48; Rom. 6:1-18; Eph. 4:1-7; 5:25-27; Col. 2:9-15

54

(Justin describes the administration of the Lord's Supper, or Eucharist.)

After we have washed him who has been convinced and has assented to our teaching, we bring him to where those who are called brethren are assembled. We offer hearty prayers in common for ourselves, for the baptized, and for everyone, everywhere. Having ended the prayers, we salute one another with a kiss. There is then brought to the president of the brethren bread and a cup of wine mixed with water. He, taking them, gives praise and glory to the Father of the universe through the name of the Son and of the Holy Spirit. He offers thanks at considerable length for our being counted worthy to receive these things from God's hands. When he has concluded the prayers and thanksgivings, all the people present express their assent by saying, "Amen." And when the president has given thanks, and all the people have expressed their assent, those whom we call deacons give to each of those present the bread and wine mixed with water. To those who are absent they carry away a portion.

THE *FIRST APOLOGY* OF JUSTIN MARTYR, CHAP. 65

LET THY BLOOD *in mercy poured,*
Let thy gracious body broken,
Be to me, O gracious Lord
Of thy boundless love the token.
Thou didst give thyself for me;
Now I give myself to thee. Amen.

A GREEK HYMN, TRANS. JOHN BROWNLIE (1907), HYMNARY

FOR REFLECTION: Luke 22:1-20; Rom. 16:16; 1 Cor. 11:23-29; 16:20; 2 Cor. 13:12; 1 Thess. 5:26; 1 Pet. 5:14

55

*(Justin Martyr continues his discussion of the Eucharist
[from Greek,* Eucharistia, *"Thanksgiving"].)*

And this food is called among us the Eucharist. No one is
allowed to partake but the person who believes that the things
we teach are true, who has been washed with the washing that
is for the remission of sins unto regeneration, and who is living
as Christ instructed. We do not receive the Eucharist as common bread and common drink. We receive it as Jesus Christ
our Savior, who having become flesh by the word of God, possessed both flesh and blood for our salvation. Likewise we have
been taught that the food that is blessed by the prayer of his
word, and from which by transformation our blood and flesh
are nourished, is the flesh and blood of that same Jesus who
was made flesh. For the apostles, in the memoirs composed
by them, which are called Gospels, have delivered to us what
was urged on them: Jesus took bread, and when he had given
thanks, said, "This do in remembrance of me, this is my body."
In the same manner, having taken the cup and given thanks, he
said, "This is my blood," and gave it to them alone.

THE *FIRST APOLOGY* OF JUSTIN MARTYR, CHAP. 66

BY THE THORNS THAT CROWNED THY BROW,
  By the spear wound and the nailing;
By the pain and death I now
  Claim, O Christ, thy love unfailing.
Thou didst give thyself for me;
Now I give myself to thee. Amen.

A GREEK HYMN, TRANS. JOHN BROWNLIE (1907), HYMNARY

✛ ✛ ✛

FOR REFLECTION: Matt. 26:14-35; Luke 22:19-20; John 13:1-30;
1 Cor. 11:23-32

56

(Justin Martyr describes the weekly worship of Christians.)

We continually remind each other of all that Christ taught and did. And the wealthy among us help the needy; we always keep together; and for all things with which we are supplied, we bless the Maker of all through his Son Jesus Christ and through the Holy Spirit. And on the day called Sunday, all who live in cities or in the country gather together to one place, and the memoirs of the apostles (i.e., the four Gospels) or the writings of the prophets are read, as long as time permits; then, when the reader has ceased, the president verbally instructs and exhorts to the imitation of these good things.

THE *FIRST APOLOGY* OF JUSTIN MARTYR, CHAP. 67

BE IN OUR MIDST; *let faith rejoice*
 Our risen Lord to view,
And make our spirits hear your voice,
 Say, "Peace be unto you."

Then, while we harken, O unfold
 The Scriptures to our mind;
Their mysteries let us now behold;
 Their hidden treasures find.

You it behooved to suffer thus,
 And to your glory rise;
Instruct, confirm, and strengthen us,
 And make your people wise. Amen.

JAMES MONTGOMERY (1771–1854), HYMNARY

FOR REFLECTION: John 15:1-8; 1 Cor. 3:1-23; 14:26-33; Eph. 1:15-23

57

(Justin Martyr continues his description of weekly worship.)

Then we all rise together and pray, and as we said before, when our prayer is ended, bread, wine, and water are brought for the Eucharist, and the president in like manner offers prayers and thanksgivings, according to his ability, and the people assent, saying, "Amen." Then there is a distribution of the bread and wine to each person. To those who are absent, a portion of the Eucharist is sent by the deacons. And those who are well-to-do, and willing, then give what each thinks appropriate. What is collected is deposited with the president, who uses it to provide for the orphans; widows; those who, through sickness or any other cause, are in want; those who are in bonds; and the strangers sojourning among us.

Sunday is the day on which we all hold our common assembly because it is the first day on which God, having wrought a change in the darkness and matter, made the world. And Jesus Christ our Savior on the same day rose from the dead. He was crucified on the day before that of Saturn (Saturday); and on the day after Saturn, which is the day of the Sun, having appeared to his apostles and disciples, he taught them these things.

THE *FIRST APOLOGY* OF JUSTIN MARTYR, CHAP. 67

COME LET US JOIN WITH ONE ACCORD
In hymns around the throne;
This is the day our rising Lord
Has made and called his own. Amen.

A *COLLECTION OF HYMNS FOR THE USE OF THE PEOPLE CALLED METHODISTS* (1889), HYMN 954

✠ ✠ ✠

FOR REFLECTION: Matt 28:1-10; Mark 16:1-11; Luke 24:1-12; John 20:1-10

ATHENAGORAS

Sometime around the year AD 177 Athenagoras (ca. 133-90), who called himself the Athenian philosopher and Christian, wrote *A Plea for the Christians*. It was an apology that defended the Christians against three accusations leveled by their pagan opponents: atheism, cannibalism, and incest. Largely because Christian worship occurred out of the public eye, and participation in the Lord's Supper was reserved for the baptized, many suspicions and accusations arose. Hatred for the Christians followed. In time, as Christian influence increased and pagan worship declined, Christians were blamed for military failures, earthquakes, diseases, famines, and invasions by the barbarians. In a later work, *On the Resurrection of the Dead,* Athenagoras defended the Christian hope of the resurrection, even as the apostle Paul had earlier done in Athens. We should lodge another major reason Christians were persecuted. Participation in the vast pagan religious structure, including the cult of emperor worship, was an expression of Roman *pietas* (collective piety), fidelity to the unity, power, and grandeur of the Roman Empire. Pagan religious practice honeycombed all facets of public and private life, including commerce, banquets and festivals, and membership in civic associations and trade guilds. Refusal to engage in and support *pietas* was quickly viewed as seditious. So because Christians refused to participate in pagan practices and to support the emperor cult, and because of rumors of repulsive things Christians did during their closed Eucharistic meetings, they were judged to be a superstition. Superstitions excessively and dangerously sought knowledge of the divine beyond reason and acceptable religious boundaries. Hence, Christians were thought to be subverting social unity, that is, to be treasonous against the empire.

We know very little about Athenagoras. He was from Athens, and like Justin, after becoming a Christian he continued to refer to himself as a philosopher. Athenagoras is recognized for his accomplished style as a writer. His statement of the Trinity, though not as refined as the doctrine would later become, is basically sound. Like Justin, Athenagoras identified some positive similarities between the philosophers and Christian beliefs. But he also observed that the philosophers often contradicted themselves because what they taught came from their own minds, not from divine revelation.

58

By presenting the doctrines to which we adhere as not being of human origin, but given and taught by God, we will convince you not to think of us as atheists. What are the doctrines in which we are reared? "I say unto you, 'Love your enemies; bless them that curse you; pray for them that persecute you; that you may be the sons of your Father who is in heaven, who causes his sun to rise on the evil and the good, and sends rain on the just and the unjust.'" Among us you will find uneducated persons, artisans, and elderly women, who, though they are unable in words to prove the fruit of our doctrine, yet by their deeds they exhibit the fruit arising from their conviction of its truth. They do not rehearse speeches but exhibit good works; when struck, they do not strike again; when robbed, they do not go to law; they give to those that ask of them and love their neighbors as themselves.

ATHENAGORAS, *A Plea for the Christians*, CHAP. 11

God, who has prepared for them that love you such good things as pass all human understanding, pour into our hearts such love towards you, that we, loving you in all things, may obtain your promises, which exceed all that we can desire, through Jesus Christ our Lord. Amen.

COLLECT, THE SIXTH SUNDAY AFTER TRINITY, IN THE BOOK OF COMMON PRAYER FOR SCOTLAND (1637)

FOR REFLECTION: Matt. 5:20-48; Luke 6:27-28; 1 Cor. 1:18-31

59

As to our not sacrificing to your gods, the Framer and Father of this universe does not need blood. He does not need the odor of burnt offerings or the fragrance of flowers and incense. For he is himself perfect fragrance, needing nothing either within or without. But the noblest sacrifice to him is for us to recognize him who stretched out and vaulted the heavens and fixed the earth in its place as a center. He gathered the water into seas and divided the light from the darkness; he adorned the sky with stars and made the earth to bring forth seed of every kind; he made animals and fashioned humankind. We believe God to be the Framer of all things. He preserves their existence and governs all of them by his knowledge and administrative skill.

ATHENAGORAS, *A PLEA FOR THE CHRISTIANS*, CHAP. 13

ALL CREATURES OF OUR GOD AND KING,
Lift up your voice and with us sing:
Alleluia! Alleluia!
You burning sun with golden beam,
You silver moon with softer gleam,

. . . .

Let all things their Creator bless,
And worship him in humbleness.
O praise him! Alleluia!
Praise, praise the Father, praise the Son,
And praise the Spirit, Three in One! Amen.

FRANCIS OF ASSISI (1182–1226), STTL, NO. 77

FOR REFLECTION: Isa. 40:21-31; Rom. 12:1-2; Col. 2:15-19; 3:1-17; Rev. 2:18-23

60

Beautiful without doubt is the world, excelling as well in its magnitude as in the arrangement of its parts. But it is not this beautiful world but its Creator that we must worship. For when any of your subjects come to you, they pay their homage to you, their rulers and lords, from whom they will obtain whatever they need. If they come upon the royal residence, they will bestow a passing glance of admiration at its beautiful structure. But it is to you yourselves that they show honor, as being "all in all."

The world is an instrument in tune and moving in well-measured time. I adore the Being who gave the world its harmony, strikes its notes, and sings its harmonious strain. But I do not worship the instrument. At musical contests the judges do not ignore the lute players and crown the lutes. As Plato says, the world is a product of divine art. I admire its beauty but worship its Creator.

ATHENAGORAS, *A PLEA FOR THE CHRISTIANS*, CHAP. 16

PRAISE THE LORD: ye heavens, adore him;
Praise him, angels, in the height;
Sun and moon, rejoice before him;
Praise him, all ye stars of light.
Praise the Lord, for he hath spoken;
Worlds his mighty voice obeyed.
Laws that never shall be broken
For their guidance he hath made. Amen.

ANONYMOUS (CA. 1801), HYMNARY

FOR REFLECTION: Ps. 19:1-10; Isa. 42:5-12; 45:5-12; Jer. 10:6-13; Col. 1:16-20

61

(Athenagoras responds to accusations against Christians that they are perpetrators of many crimes.)

The lives of Christians are directed toward God as their rule, so that each one among us may be blameless and irreproachable before him. We will not entertain even the thought of the slightest sin. For if we believed that we should live only the present life, then we might be suspected of sinning, being enslaved to the flesh and blood, or mastered by gain and carnal desire. But we know that God is witness to what we think and what we say, both by night and by day, and that he, being himself light, sees all things in our hearts.

We are persuaded that when we are removed from the present life, we shall live another life, better than the present one, and heavenly, not earthly (since we shall abide near God and with God, free from all change or suffering in the soul). For these reasons it is unlikely that we should choose to do evil or deliver ourselves over to the great Judge to be punished.

ATHENAGORAS, *A PLEA FOR THE CHRISTIANS*, CHAP. 31

APPROACH, MY SOUL, the mercy seat,
Where Jesus answers prayer;
There humbly fall before his feet,
For none can perish there.

Thy promise is my only plea,
With this I venture nigh;
Thou callest burdened souls to thee,
And such, O Lord, am I.

JOHN NEWTON (1725–1807), HYMNARY

✚ ✚ ✚

FOR REFLECTION: Rom. 8:1-16; 1 Cor. 15:13-20, 34-58; 1 John 3:1-11

62

We are so far from practicing promiscuous behavior that it is not lawful for us to indulge even a lustful look. "For," says our Lord, "he that looks on a woman to lust after her has committed adultery already in his heart." We, then, who are forbidden to look at anything more than that for which God formed the eyes, which were intended to be a light for us, and to whom a wanton look is adultery (the eyes being made for other purposes), and who must account for our very thoughts, how can anyone doubt that we practice self-control? For our primary accountability lies not with human laws, which an evil person can evade, but we have a law that makes the measure of moral uprightness to consist of treating our neighbor as ourselves.

ATHENAGORAS, *A Plea for the Christians*, CHAP. 32

O Sovereign and Almighty Lord, who sits on the cherubim and is glorified by the seraphim, who has made the heavens and adorned them with choirs of stars, who has placed a host of angels in the highest heavens to sing your praise forever, we beseech you to repel the dark assaults of sin from our understanding and to gladden our minds with the divine radiance of your Holy Spirit. Pardon all our sins in your abundant and unsearchable goodness, through the grace, mercy, and love of your only begotten Son. Amen.

THE DIVINE LITURGY OF THE HOLY APOSTLE AND EVANGELIST MARK
(BEFORE AD 200)

FOR REFLECTION: Matt. 5:27-32; 1 Cor. 10:1-14; Gal. 5:13-26

63

Since such is our character, how can anyone of a sound mind say that we are murderers? We, who believe that to see men put to death in contests of gladiators and wild beasts is much the same as killing them, have repudiated such spectacles lest we should contract guilt and pollution; how can we commit murder? And when we say that women who use drugs to bring on abortion commit murder, and will give an account to God for the abortion, by what rationale could we commit murder? It does not belong to the same person to regard the fetus in the womb as a person, an object of God's care, and then, when it is born, to kill it. We do not abandon an infant to the elements because those who expose infants are guilty of infanticide.

ATHENAGORAS, *A PLEA FOR THE CHRISTIANS*, CHAP. 35

BE THOU MY WISDOM, and thou my true Word;
I ever with thee, and thou with me, Lord;

. . . .

Thou and thou only, first in my heart,
High King of heaven, my Treasure thou art.
High King of heaven, my victory won,
May I reach heaven's joys, bright heaven's Sun!
Heart of my own heart, whatever befall,
Still be my Vision, O Ruler of all. Amen.

IRISH HYMN (CA. EIGHTH CENTURY AD), TRANS. MARY E. BYRNE (1905),
STTL, NO. 460

FOR REFLECTION: Matt. 5:13-16, 21-24; Rom. 13:7-14; 2 Cor. 6:14-18; Eph. 5:1-21

64

(Athenagoras discusses the resurrection of the dead.)

God's power is sufficient to raise the dead. This is proved by the creation of our bodies. Before humans existed, God chose to create them and all their original component elements. Therefore, when they are corrupted by death, whatever the cause, God will raise them again with equal ease. For like the original creation, this, too, is possible for God. The divine power that could give shape to shapeless matter and give life to what formerly had no life can reunite what is dissolved and raise up what is laid low. God can restore the dead to life again and transform the corruptible into incorruption.

ATHENAGORAS, *ON THE RESURRECTION OF THE DEAD*, CHAP. 3

Almighty God, who by your holy apostle has taught us to set our affection on things above: Grant us so to labor in this life that we may ever be mindful of our citizenship in those heavenly places where our Savior Christ has gone before; who lives and reigns with you and the Holy Spirit, ever one God, world without end. Amen.

COLLECT, ASCENSION EVE, IN THE SCOTTISH BOOK OF COMMON PRAYER (1929)

FOR REFLECTION: John 11:1-27; Acts 2:22-36; 1 Cor. 15:1-58

THEOPHILUS OF ANTIOCH

Around the year AD 180, Theophilus (d. ca. AD 183-85), bishop of Antioch, wrote three treatises to his friend Autolycus in an effort to convince him to become a Christian. He wrote other books that have been lost. Theophilus was reared a pagan but became a Christian by meditating on the Scriptures. Around the year 169 he succeeded Cornelius as bishop of Antioch. Historian of doctrines Justo González says Theophilus was the first Christian author to use the term "trinity" when speaking of the Father, Son, and Holy Spirit.* According to Theophilus, only those of a pure soul can see God.

Theophilus had a Greek education. But unlike some of the other apologists, he was not schooled in Greek philosophy. He claimed no mastery of rhetoric. He had no regard for what the philosophers taught about God, thinking their opinions and those of the poets were so contradictory as to be worthless. Because the philosophers and poets did not have the benefit of revelation, Theophilus taught, they issued useless ideas. Unlike the foolish stories and fables the pagans embraced, the Old Testament prophets were inspired by the Holy Spirit. Holy and righteous, they were made wise by God.

Theophilus's style of writing is described as lively, imaginative, and original; his diction as elegant and ornate. Style is on display as Theophilus lampoons pagan worship, surgically exposes the contradictory genealogies of the deities, and scorns their shameful immorality (Saturn is a cannibal, Jupiter is incestuous and adulterous, Hercules burns himself, Bacchus is drunk and raging, and Apollo fears and flees from Achilles). At many points, his keen analysis becomes humorous (Egyptians are depicted worshipping washpots).

---

*Justo González, *A History of Christian Thought* (Nashville: Abingdon Press, 1970), 1:117.

65

To see God, the eyes of your soul must be capable of seeing, and the ears of your heart able to hear. Those who look with physical eyes see only earthly objects and what concerns this life. Humans discriminate between things that differ, whether light or darkness, white or black, deformed or beautiful, well-proportioned and symmetrical or disproportioned and awkward, or monstrous or mutilated. In like manner, by the sense of hearing we discriminate between sharp, deep, or sweet sounds. The same holds true for the eyes of the soul and the ears of the heart. By them, Christians are able to behold God. All persons have eyes, but in some people their eyes are overspread with cataracts and they cannot see the light of God.

THEOPHILUS OF ANTIOCH, *To Autolycus*, BK. 1, CHAP. 2

HOLY FATHER, GREAT CREATOR,
 Source of mercy, love, and peace,
Look upon the Mediator,
 Clothe us with his righteousness;
Heavenly Father,
 Through the Savior hear and bless.

. . . .

God the Lord, through every nation
 Let thy wondrous mercies shine!
In the song of thy salvation
 Every tongue and race combine!
Great Jehovah,
 Form our hearts and make them thine. Amen.

ALEXANDER V. GRISWOLD (1766–1843), HYMNARY

✠ ✠ ✠

FOR REFLECTION: Pss. 46:10; 139:1-18; Prov. 1:7; 2:3-9; 9:1-6; John 3:1-13; 1 Cor. 1:19-25

66

God is Lord, because he rules over the universe; Father, because he is before all things; Fashioner and Maker, because he is Creator and Maker of the universe; the Highest, because of his being above all; and Almighty, because he himself rules and embraces all. For the heights of heaven, the depths of the abysses, and the ends of the earth are in his hands. The heavens are his work, the earth is his creation, and the sea is his handiwork; humankind is his formation and his image; sun, moon, and stars are his elements, made for signs, seasons, days, and years, that they may serve humans; and all things God has made out of things that were not, into things that are, in order that through his works his greatness may be known and understood.

THEOPHILUS OF ANTIOCH, *To Autolycus*, BK. 1, CHAP. 4

WE PRAISE YOU, O GOD, OUR REDEEMER, Creator;
  In grateful devotion our tribute we bring;
We lay it before you; we kneel and adore you;
  We bless your holy name: glad praises we sing.

. . . .

With voices united our praises we offer,
  Our songs of thanksgiving to you we now raise;
Your strong arm will guide us; our God is beside us;
  To you, our great Redeemer, forever be praise! Amen.

JULIA C. CORY (1882–1963), HYMNARY

✦ ✦ ✦

FOR REFLECTION: Pss. 77:14; 89:8-13; 147:5, 16, 18; Isa. 45:7-18; 57:11-19; Amos 4:13; Acts 14:15-26; Rom. 1:20

67

Just as the soul of a person is not seen, it being invisible to humans, but is perceived through the motion of the body, even so God cannot be seen by human eyes but is beheld and perceived through his providence and works. Similarly, when someone sees a ship on the sea, rigged and in sail, and making for the harbor, he will no doubt infer that a pilot is steering the ship. Even so, we must see that God is the Governor and Pilot of the whole universe, even though he is not visible to physical eyes. If a person cannot look upon the sun, a small heavenly body, because of its exceeding heat and power, shall not a mortal be much less able to face the glory of God, which is inexpressible? For, as the pomegranate contains in its rind many covered seeds, and has within it many compartments, so the whole creation is contained by the Spirit of God. An earthly king is believed to exist, even though he is not seen by everyone, for he is recognized by his laws and ordinances, authorities, forces, and statues. Are you unwilling to recognize God by his works and mighty deeds?

THEOPHILUS OF ANTIOCH, *To Autolycus*, BK. 1, CHAP. 5

O Lord, how manifold the works
In wisdom wrought by thee;
The wealth of thy creation fills
The earth and mighty sea.

Let God rejoice in all his works,
And let his works proclaim
Forevermore their Maker's praise,
And glorify his name. Amen.

THE PSALTER: WITH RESPONSIVE READINGS (1912), NO. 288, HYMNARY

✦✦✦

FOR REFLECTION: Job 37:6-24; Pss. 37:7-10; 65:9-13; 98:6-8; 104:10-34; 111:1-10; Matt. 6:26-34

68

This is my God, the Lord of all, who alone stretched out heaven and established the breadth of the earth under it; who stirs the deep recesses of the sea and makes its waves roar; who rules its power and stills the tumult of its waves; who founded the earth upon the waters and gave a spirit to nourish it; whose breath gives light to the whole, which would utterly fail if he were to withdraw his breath. By him you speak, O Autolycus; by his breath you breathe, yet you do not know him because of the blindness of your soul and the hardness of your heart. But if you will, you may be healed. Entrust yourself to the Physician, and he will restore the eyes of your soul and of your heart. Who is this Physician? God, who heals and makes alive through his word and wisdom.

THEOPHILUS OF ANTIOCH, *To Autolycus*, BK. 1, CHAP. 7

FOR THE BEAUTY OF THE EARTH,
For the glory of the skies,
For the love that from our birth
Over and around us lies.

. . . .

For yourself, best gift divine,
To the world so freely given,
Agent of God's grand design:
Peace on earth and joy in heaven.

Christ, our Lord, to you we raise
This, our hymn of grateful praise. Amen.

FOLLIOTT PIERPOINT (1835–1917), HYMNARY

✦ ✦ ✦

FOR REFLECTION: Pss. 23:1-5; 33:6; 65:6; 74:16-17; 90:2; Matt. 9:27-31; 15:30-31; John 7:32-44; Col. 1:14-17

69

Faith is the leading principle in all matters. For what husband-man can reap, unless he first trust his seed to the earth? Or who can cross the sea, unless he first entrusts himself to the boat and the pilot? And what sick person can be healed, unless first he trusts himself to the care of the physician? And what knowledge or art can anyone learn, unless he first apply and entrust himself to the teacher? If, then, the husbandman trusts the earth, the sailor the boat, and the sick the physician, will you not place confidence in God, even when you already owe so much to his hand? For first he created you out of nothing, brought you into existence, and introduced you into this life. Can you not believe that the God who made you is able also to recreate you in the resurrection?

THEOPHILUS OF ANTIOCH, *To Autolycus*, BK. 1, CHAP. 8

O GOD, the strength of all who put their trust in you: Mercifully accept our prayers; and because in our weakness we can do nothing good without you, give us the help of your grace, that in keeping your commandments we may please you both in will and deed; through Jesus Christ our Lord, who lives and reigns with you and the Holy Spirit, one God, forever and ever. Amen.

"SIXTH SUNDAY AFTER THE EPIPHANY," COLLECTS: CONTEMPORARY, IN BCP

FOR REFLECTION: Pss. 18:1-29; 37:3-39; Matt. 6:25-34; Luke 12:22-32; Heb. 11:1–12:2

70

It seems to me absurd that sculptors and carvers, painters, or molders should design and paint, carve, mold, and prepare gods, who, once they are produced by the artificers, are reckoned of no value. But as soon as they are purchased and placed in some so-called temple or in some house, not only do those who bought them sacrifice to them, but also those who made and sold them come with much devotion, implements of sacrifice, and libations to worship them. And they reckon them to be gods, not seeing that they are still just as they were when they were fabricated from stone, brass, wood, color, or some other material.

When Greeks and Romans give the histories and genealogies of the so-called gods, they think of them as humans at their births. But afterward they call them gods and worship them, not reflecting or understanding that, when born, the gods were the same humans as those in the histories and genealogies.

THEOPHILUS OF ANTIOCH, *To Autolycus*, BK. 2, CHAP. 2

ALMIGHTY GOD, give us grace to cast away the works of darkness and put on the armor of light, now in the time of this mortal life in which your Son Jesus Christ came to visit us in great humility; that in the last day, when he shall come again in his glorious majesty to judge both the living and the dead, we may rise to the life immortal; through him who lives and reigns with you and the Holy Spirit, one God, now and forever. Amen.

"FIRST SUNDAY OF ADVENT," COLLECTS: CONTEMPORARY, IN BCP

FOR REFLECTION: Pss. 96:5; 115:4-8; 135:15-18; Isa. 44:9-20; 46:1-7; Jer. 10:11-15

71

It would be no great thing if God were to make the world out of things that already exist. Even a human artisan, when he obtains material, makes of it what he pleases. But the power of God is manifested in this, that out of things that are not, he makes whatever he pleases. Bestowing life and mobility is the prerogative of God alone. Humans can create lifeless images. But humans cannot give reason, breath, and feeling to the gods they create. God alone has this power, and this in excess. He creates humans and endows them with reason, life, and sensation. As in all these things, God is more powerful than humans, so also in the following: out of things that are not, God creates things that are, and he creates whatever pleases him.

THEOPHILUS OF ANTIOCH, *To Autolycus*, BK. 2, CHAP. 4

O MERCIFUL CREATOR, your hand is open wide to satisfy the needs of every living creature: Make us always thankful for your loving providence; and grant that we, remembering the account that we must one day give, may be faithful stewards of your good gifts; through Jesus Christ our Lord, who with you and the Holy Spirit lives and reigns, one God, forever and ever. Amen.

"FOR STEWARDSHIP OF CREATION," COLLECTS: CONTEMPORARY, IN BCP

FOR REFLECTION: Pss. 33:6; 148:5; John 1:1-5; Rom. 1:19-20; 4:17; Col. 1:16; Heb. 11:3

THE "SCHOOL" OF
ALEXANDRIA

Before the New Testament era ended, churches in some leading cities of the empire had gained special importance for the Christian mission. Jerusalem and Antioch are prominent in the book of Acts. As the gospel spread, other cities became leading centers of missionary work and theological energy. In time, Carthage, Constantinople, and Rome would come to fill these roles. In the second century, the church in Egypt—the "breadbasket of the empire"—particularly the city of Alexandria, became a major Christian center for evangelism, Christian teaching and learning, and martyrdom. Some of the most influential early fathers were based in Alexandria. They constitute a "school" because of distinct similarities in how they understood the faith. The Alexandrian fathers shepherded the Christian flock, defended the faith before its pagan and Jewish opponents, and sometimes died as martyrs. Some of the church's bishops were major voices in decisive church decisions.

Traditionally, the church in Egypt has been associated with John Mark, initially a missionary companion of Paul and Barnabas and named as author of the second gospel. The persecuted Christian Coptic Orthodox Church of Egypt teaches that Mark preached the gospel in Egypt during the reign of

Emperor Nero (AD 54-68) and established the church there. The church in Egypt is properly proud of Athanasius (ca. AD 296–373), who played a decisive role in defining orthodoxy at the Council of Nicaea.

We will draw from three fathers associated with the church and school in Alexandria.

CLEMENT OF ALEXANDRIA

As the third century dawned, no city in the Roman Empire rivaled Alexandria, Egypt, as a center of learning and culture. Partly because of its geographical location, the city was a scene of a cosmopolitan convergence of races, religions, and philosophies. The city was one of the empire's great trading centers. Established in 332 or 321 BC by Alexander the Great, the city became famous for its astonishing cultural accomplishments. Its famous library, whose directors were among the world's most accomplished scholars, housed seven hundred thousand volumes. The city's museum functioned as a university that attracted a community of eminent scholars. Philosophy and the sciences flourished. Alexandria was home to the most enlightened colony of dispersed Jews. They absorbed the atmosphere of Greek philosophy (especially Plato) and science and interpreted their religion under Greek auspices. Here the Jewish Scriptures were translated into Greek to form the Septuagint. The city provided an intellectual home for Philo, one of the greatest Jewish philosophers of all time, a sort of Jewish Plato. Alexandria was also one of the chief centers of Gnostic speculation, creatively combining the beliefs of numerous religions and mythologies.

Although there were notable and intense persecutions, Christians flourished in Alexandria. Not surprisingly, the city became an intellectual center for formulating comprehensive explanations of the Christian faith for the church and for inquiring pagans. Late in the second century, under the leadership of some highly gifted Christians, a catechetical school called the Didascalia was created to instruct Christian converts. In addition to elementary and advanced instruction for Christians, lectures were given to pagan auditors. In time, the School of Alexandria became the intellectual powerhouse of the Christian mission at a time when the church in Rome was a pupil by comparison, well behind the church in North Africa.

The School of Alexandria would come to interpret the Christian faith in ways that would become stoutly opposed in other parts of the church. A Christian teacher named Pantaenus (d. ca. AD 212), formerly a Stoic philosopher, was the school's founder. His successor was Titus Flavius Clemens, known to the church as Clement of Alexandria (d. ca. AD 215). Probably born in Athens, Clement early became a Christian convert. He sought Christian instruction in Italy, Syria, and Palestine. His search ended when he met Pantaenus. Around AD 202, persecution forced Clement to leave Alexandria.

Through oral instruction and his writings, Clement became one of the foremost teachers of the early church. He had an appreciation for Greek philosophy, especially Plato, not shared by some other fathers. Clement employed reason as a tool for articulating the faith and for interpreting the Bible but only as an instrument in the service of faith. For him, the use of reason is a process of faith seeking understanding under the Spirit's guidance. Clement's writings now in our possession are *Exhortation to the Heathen*, the *Instructor*, *Stromata (Miscellanies)*, and *Who Is the Rich Man That Shall Be Saved?* Another work, *Exhortation to the Newly Baptized*, is often attributed to Clement. But its authenticity is too doubtful to be included here.

72

Jesus Christ is the New Song that speedily loosens the bitter bondage of tyrannizing demons. The New Song leads us back to the mild and loving yoke of piety. It recalls to heaven those that had been cast prostrate to earth. Behold the might of the New Song! It has made humans out of stones, humans out of beasts. Those, moreover, that were as dead, not being partakers of the true life, have come to life again, simply by listening to the Song. This Song also composed the universe into melodious order, and tuned the discord of the elements to harmonious arrangement, so that the whole world might become harmony. By the Holy Spirit, Christ the New Song tuned the universe, especially the human body and soul—the universe in miniature.

CLEMENT OF ALEXANDRIA, *EXHORTATION TO THE HEATHEN*, CHAP. 1

O SING A NEW SONG TO THE LORD,
  For wonders he has done:
His right hand and his holy arm
  Him victory has won.

. . . .

Let all the earth unto the Lord
  Send forth a joyful noise;
Lift up your voice aloud to him,
  Sing praises, and rejoice.

With harp, with harp, and voice of psalms,
  Unto Jehovah sing:
With trumpets, cornets, gladly sound
  Before the Lord the King. Amen.

SCOTTISH PSALTER (1650), HYMNARY

✦✦✦

FOR REFLECTION: Exod. 15:1-19; Pss. 40:1-11; 42:7-11; 96:1-13; Isa. 35:3-10; Col. 3:16; Rev. 5:1-10

73

(Clement has lampooned the hymns sung upon initiation into some pagan mysteries. These he contrasts with the music of the Lord.)

After his own image the Lord made of humankind a beautiful breathing instrument of music. And the Lord himself, the celestial Word, is the all-harmonious, melodious, holy Instrument of God. What, then, does this Instrument—the Word of God, the Lord, the New Song—desire? To open the eyes of the blind, unstop the ears of the deaf, lead the lame or the erring to righteousness, exhibit God to the foolish, put a stop to corruption, conquer death, and reconcile disobedient children to their father. This Instrument of God loves humankind. The Lord pities, instructs, exhorts, admonishes, saves, and shields, and of his bounty promises us the kingdom of heaven as a reward for learning. The only advantage he reaps is that we are saved. Wickedness feeds on the destruction of people; but truth, like the bee, harming nothing, delights only in salvation.

CLEMENT OF ALEXANDRIA, *EXHORTATION TO THE HEATHEN*, CHAP. 1

HOLY ARE YOU, O God our Father, truly the only one, of whom the whole family in heaven and earth is named. Holy are you, Eternal Son, through whom all things were made. Holy are you, Holy, Eternal Spirit, through whom all things are sanctified. May your grace be with us, O Lord; purge away our impurities, and sanctify our lips. And because of all your gifts and favors to us, we shall ascribe to you praise, honor, thanksgiving, and adoration, now, always, and forever and ever. Amen.

ADAEUS AND MARIS, THE LITURGY OF THE BLESSED APOSTLES (CA. AD 150)

✛ ✛ ✛

FOR REFLECTION: Pss. 8:1-9; 25:8-10; 33:5; 46:1-11; Isa. 2:3; 63:7; Matt. 7:11; James 1:17-20; Rev. 5:9; 14:3; 15:3

74

The New Song, this Word, this Christ, the cause of both our being at first and of our well-being now, this very Word, has now come as human. He alone is both God and human—the Author of all blessings. By him we, being taught to live well, are sent on our way to life eternal. For, according to that inspired apostle of the Lord, "the grace of God that brings salvation has appeared to all people, teaching us, that, denying ungodliness and worldly lusts, we should live soberly, righteously, and godly, in this present world; looking for the blessed hope, and appearing of the glory of the great God and our Savior Jesus Christ." He is the Word who in the beginning bestowed on us life as Creator when he formed us. Then he taught us how to live well when he appeared as our Teacher, so that, as God, he might afterward guide us to the life that never ends. He did not now for the first time pity us for our error, for he pitied us from the beginning. But now, at his coming, lost as we were, he has gained our salvation.

CLEMENT OF ALEXANDRIA, *EXHORTATION TO THE HEATHEN*, CHAP. 1

ALMIGHTY GOD, give us grace that we may cast away the works of darkness and put on us armor of light, now in the time of this mortal life, in which your Son Jesus Christ came to visit us in great humility; that in the last day, when he shall come again in his glorious Majesty to judge both the living and the dead, we may rise to the life immortal; through him who lives and reigns with you and the Holy Spirit, now and ever. Amen.

COLLECT, THE FIRST SUNDAY IN ADVENT,
IN THE SCOTTISH BOOK OF COMMON PRAYER (1929)

FOR REFLECTION: Isa. 13:10; 42:10; John 1:1-5; 2 Cor. 5:1-19; Gal. 3:7-14; **Titus 2:11-13**; 1 Pet. 3:8-9

75

Speaking by the prophet Isaiah, God says, "There is an inheritance for those who serve the LORD." Noble and desirable is this inheritance: not gold, not silver, not raiment, which the moth assails, not things of earth that are assailed by the robber whose eye is dazzled by worldly wealth; but it is that treasure of salvation to which we must hasten by becoming lovers of the Word. This is the inheritance with which the eternal covenant of God invests us, conveying the everlasting gift of grace. Thus our loving Father—the true Father—ceases not to exhort, admonish, train, and love us. For he ceases not to save, and advise the best course for us: "Become righteous," says the Lord.

CLEMENT OF ALEXANDRIA, *EXHORTATION TO THE HEATHEN*, CHAP. 10

O SOVEREIGN AND ALMIGHTY LORD, grant that we may end our lives as Christians, acceptable to you and without sin. Be pleased to give us part and lot with all your saints. Pardon all our sins in your abundant and unsearchable goodness, through the grace, mercy, and love of your only begotten Son, through whom and with whom be glory and power to you, with the all-holy, good, and life-giving Spirit. Amen.

THE DIVINE LITURGY OF THE HOLY APOSTLE AND EVANGELIST MARK
(BEFORE AD 200)

FOR REFLECTION: Isa. 54:17; 55:1; Acts 20:28-32; 26:15-18; Eph. 1:3-14

76

All you that thirst, come to the water; and you that have no money, come, and buy and drink without money. He invites us to the font of cleansing, to salvation, to illumination. He all but cries out and says, "The land I give you, and the sea, my child, and heaven, too; and all the living creatures in them I freely bestow on you. Only, O child, thirst for your Father; God shall be revealed to you without price; his truth is not bought and sold like merchandise."

CLEMENT OF ALEXANDRIA, *EXHORTATION TO THE HEATHEN*, CHAP. 10

O GOD, you have prepared for those who love you such good things as surpass our understanding: Pour into our hearts such love toward you, that we, loving you in all things and above all things, may obtain your promises, which exceed all that we can desire; through Jesus Christ our Lord, who lives and reigns with you and the Holy Spirit, one God, forever and ever. Amen.

"SIXTH SUNDAY OF EASTER," COLLECTS: CONTEMPORARY, IN BCP

FOR REFLECTION: Isa. 55:1-3; John 4:1-26; 6:35; 7:37-39; Eph. 2:5-10

77

Contemplate for a while God's kindness. Adam, seduced by lusts and disobeying his Father, was found fettered to sin. The Lord then wished to release him from his bonds, and having clothed himself in flesh—O divine mystery!—vanquished the serpent and enslaved the tyrant death. Most marvelous of all, humans who had been deceived by pleasure and bound fast by corruption had their hands unloosed and were set free. O heavenly wonder! The Lord was laid low, and man was lifted up. Therefore, because the Word himself has come to us from heaven, we need not, I am certain, go anymore in search of human learning to Athens and the rest of Greece and to Ionia. For if we have as our teacher him that filled the universe with his holy energies in creation, salvation, kindness, law, prophecy, and teaching, then we have the Teacher from whom all instruction comes.

CLEMENT OF ALEXANDRIA, *EXHORTATION TO THE HEATHEN*, CHAP. 11

ALLELUIA, ALLELUIA, ALLELUIA!
The strife is o'er, the battle done;
The victory of life is won;
The song of triumph has begun.
Alleluia!

The powers of death have done their worst,
But Christ their legions has dispersed.
Let shouts of holy joy outburst.
Alleluia! Amen.

ANONYMOUS, IN *SYMPHONIA SIRENUM SELECTARUM* (1695),
TRANS. FRANCIS POTT (1861), HYMNARY

FOR REFLECTION: Gen. 1:1-5; John 1:12-14; 17:1-26; Gal. 3:28; 6:15

78

"Sweet is the Word that gives us light, precious above gold and gems; it is to be desired above honey and the honeycomb." For how can it be other than desirable, since the Word has filled with light the mind that had once been buried in darkness? For just as had the sun not existed, night would have brooded over the universe. Even so, had we not known the Word and been illuminated by him, we would have been in no way different from fowls that are being fed, fattened in darkness, and nourished for death. Let us then put away all ignorance of the truth, and removing the darkness that obstructs, let us contemplate the only true God, raising our voice in this hymn of praise: "Hail, O light! For in us, buried in darkness, shut up in the shadow of death, light has shone forth from heaven, purer than the sun, sweeter than life here below."

CLEMENT OF ALEXANDRIA, *EXHORTATION TO THE HEATHEN*, CHAP. 11

SING MY SOUL HIS WONDROUS LOVE,
Who from that bright throne above,
Ever watchful o'er our race,
Still to man extends his grace.

. . . .

God, the merciful and good,
Bought us with the Savior's blood,
And, to make our safety sure,
Guides us by his Spirit pure. Amen.

ANONYMOUS (1800), HYMNARY

✦ ✦ ✦

FOR REFLECTION: Ps. 19:10; Matt. 9:36; 14:14; 18:10-14; Luke 7:11-16; John 10:7-15

79

The "Sun of Righteousness" has changed sunset into sunrise and through the cross has brought death to life. And having wrenched humans from destruction, he has raised them to the skies, transforming mortality into immortality and translating earth to heaven. He, the Husbandman of God, has bestowed on us the truly great, divine, and inalienable inheritance of the Father. He sanctified us by heavenly teaching, putting his laws into our minds and writing them on our hearts. And though God needs nothing, let us render to him the grateful recompense of a thankful heart and of piety.

Let the light then shine in our hidden part, that is, the heart; and let the beams of knowledge arise to reveal and irradiate the hidden inner person, the disciple of him who is the Light, the friend and fellow heir of Christ. Especially now that we have come to know the most precious and venerable name of the good Father, who to a pious and good child gives gentle counsel and commands what is beneficial for his child.

CLEMENT OF ALEXANDRIA, *EXHORTATION TO THE HEATHEN*, CHAP. 11

THE DAY OF RESURRECTION!
Earth, tell it out abroad;
The Passover of gladness,
The Passover of God.
From death to life eternal,
From earth to the sky,
Our Christ has brought us over,
With hymns of victory. Amen.

JOHN OF DAMASCUS (CA. AD 675–749), TRANS. JOHN M. NEALE (1862),
HYMNARY

FOR REFLECTION: Jer. 31:31-34; Luke 1:68-79; John 12:42-50; 1 Cor. 15:53-54; Eph. 1:3-8; 2:13-22; 5:8, 13; 1 Thess. 4:1-18; Heb. 8:10-12

80

O this holy and blessed power by which God has fellowship with humans! Better far, then, is it to become at once the imitator and the servant of the best of all beings; for only by holy service will anyone be able to imitate God and to serve and worship him. The heavenly and truly divine love comes to humans thus: when in the soul itself the spark of true goodness, kindled by the Divine Word, is able to burst forth into flame, and when, what is of the highest importance, salvation runs parallel with sincere obedience, that is, choice and life being yoked together. Therefore this exhortation from the truth alone, like the most faithful of our friends, abides with us till our last breath. It is to the whole and perfect spirit of the soul the kind attendant as we ascend to heaven.

CLEMENT OF ALEXANDRIA, *EXHORTATION TO THE HEATHEN*, CHAP. 11

ALMIGHTY GOD, whose Son our Savior Jesus Christ is the Light of the World: Grant that your people, illumined by your Word and Sacraments, may shine with the radiance of Christ's glory, that he may be known, worshipped, and obeyed to the ends of the earth; through Jesus Christ our Lord, who with you and the Holy Spirit lives and reigns, one God, now and forever. Amen.

"SECOND SUNDAY AFTER THE EPIPHANY," COLLECTS: CONTEMPORARY, **IN** BCP

FOR REFLECTION: Rom. 8:27-31; 1 Cor. 13:12; 2 Cor. 3:16-18; Eph. 3:8-21; 2 Pet. 1:1-6; 1 John 3:1-3

81

What, then, is the exhortation I give to you? I urge you to be saved. This is what Christ desires. In a word, he will freely bestow life on you. And who is he? Briefly learn that he is the Word of Truth, the Word of incorruption that regenerates persons by bringing them back to the truth. He is the goad that urges us toward salvation. He expels destruction and exhausts death of its power. He builds up the temple of God in humans so God may take up his abode in them. Therefore, cleanse the temple; pleasures and amusements abandon to the winds and to the fire as a fading flower. But wisely cultivate the fruits of self-control, and present yourself to God as an offering so that you may be rendered worthy of the kingdom of God.

CLEMENT OF ALEXANDRIA, *EXHORTATION TO THE HEATHEN*, CHAP. 11

ALMIGHTY GOD, whom truly to know is everlasting life: Grant us so perfectly to know your Son Jesus Christ to be the way, the truth, and the life, that we may steadfastly follow his steps in the way that leads to eternal life; through Jesus Christ your Son our Lord, who lives and reigns with you, in the unity of the Holy Spirit, one God, forever and ever. Amen.

"FIFTH SUNDAY OF EASTER," COLLECTS: CONTEMPORARY, IN BCP

FOR REFLECTION: Luke 1:68-79; 2:11-34; John 1:15-18; 3:16-17; 10:7-27, 30-36; Rom. 5:1-11; 1 Pet. 2:4-25

82

Jesus, who is eternal, the one great High Priest of the one God, his Father, prays for and exhorts us: "I call on the whole human race, whose Creator I am, by the will of the Father. Come to me that you may be given your proper place under the one God and the one Word of God. For to you I grant the enjoyment of immortality. For I want to impart this grace to you, bestowing on you the perfect benefit of immortality. And I confer on you both the Word and the knowledge of God, my complete self. This I am; this God wills; this is symphony; this is the harmony of the Father; this is the Son; this is Christ; this is the Word of God, the arm of the Lord, the power of the universe, and the will of the Father. I anoint you with the balm of faith, by which you throw off corruption, and I show you the pure form of righteousness by which to ascend to God. Come to me, all you that labor and are heavy laden, and I will give you rest. Take my yoke upon you, and learn of me; for I am meek and lowly in heart: and you shall find rest to your souls. For my yoke is easy, and my burden light."

CLEMENT OF ALEXANDRIA, *EXHORTATION TO THE HEATHEN*, CHAP. 12

O GOD, the strength of all who put their trust in you: Mercifully accept our prayers; and because in our weakness we can do nothing good without you, give us the help of your grace, that in keeping your commandments we may please you both in will and deed; through Jesus Christ our Lord, who lives and reigns with you and the Holy Spirit, one God, forever and ever. Amen.

"SIXTH SUNDAY AFTER THE EPIPHANY," COLLECTS: CONTEMPORARY, IN BCP

FOR REFLECTION: Matt. 11:25-30; John 15:1-17; 17:1-5; Gal. 6:7-8; 1 Tim. 4:8; 6:6

83

Having yoked the team of Christians to God, the Good Chari-oteer, who is Christ, directs his chariot to immortality, driving on to heaven. A sight most beautiful to the Father is his eternal Son crowned with victory. Let us aspire, then, after what is good; let us become God-loving people and gain the greatest of all things that cannot be harmed—God and eternal life. Our helper is the Word; let us put all our confidence in him. And never let us be visited by a craving for silver, gold, and glory as strong as our love for the Word of Truth himself. For it will be displeasing to God if we value least those things that are worth most, and value most the clear outrages and total impiety of fol-ly, ignorance, thoughtlessness, and idolatry.

CLEMENT OF ALEXANDRIA, *EXHORTATION TO THE HEATHEN*, CHAP. 12

JOIN ALL THE NAMES *of love and power*
That ever men or angels bore;
All are too mean to speak his worth,
Or set Emmanuel's glory forth.

. . . .

My bright Example and my Guide,
I would be walking near your side;
O let me never run astray,
Nor follow the forbidden way!

. . . .

Aspire, my soul, to glorious deeds,
The Captain of salvation leads;
March on, nor fear to win the day,
Though death and hell obstruct the way. Amen.

ISAAC WATTS (1674–1748), HYMNARY

✦ ✦ ✦

FOR REFLECTION: Phil. 3:13-21; Col. 3:2-6; Rev. 14:1-7; 15:1-4; 19:1-16

ORIGEN

In Origen of Alexandria (ca. AD 185–ca. 254), surnamed Adamantius (Man of Steel), we meet one of the towering, though sometimes controversial, early fathers. From an early age he was a passionate disciple of Jesus Christ. Gifted with brilliance, his highest goal was to be a living image of Jesus Christ—what he called being a statue of Christ formed by Christian excellence. All of Origen's formidable abilities were aimed at expounding the Scriptures and clearly teaching the whole doctrine of Christ. The purpose of the Scriptures, Origen taught, is to lead persons to redemption through Jesus Christ and to lead the converted to Christian maturation.

Origen was probably born and reared in intellectually and religiously rich Alexandria. The city was a center for Christian learning, a fertile context for Jewish thought, and an enthusiastic patron of science and Greek philosophy, especially Plato. Origen lived when the formulation of Christian orthodoxy was still in some respects unsettled and when the church was still experiencing cycles of brutal oppression.

Born of Christian parents, Origen became the most famous student of Clement of Alexandria. His first theological training came from his father, Leonidas, who was martyred in 202 or 203. Later, Origen became a student of Pantaenus, founder of the catechetical school in Alexandria. Origen became Clement's student when the latter succeeded Pantaenus. At age seventeen he was asked to teach grammar in the catechetical school. A year later, because of Origen's precocious mind and grasp of the Christian faith, Bishop Demetrius assigned him head of the school to succeed Clement.

Though not a presbyter (priest), Origen became an eminently successful teacher of the Scriptures and Christian theology. He used his extensive knowledge of Greco-Roman religion and philosophy to expose the errors of paganism and to defend the gospel against critics. Origen had the intellectual and theological equipment to defend the faith against Gnostics and Marcion (who wanted to separate the Old Testament from the New) and to give to them a carefully considered response. He placed his considerable knowledge of Greek philosophy in service to the church and used it to expose what he believed to be philosophy's shortcomings. He contributed significantly to the development of the doctrine of the Trinity.

Critics of Origen believe his reliance on Neoplatonism did not serve Christian theology well in some important ways. It colored his interpretation of Scripture and his explanation of Christian doctrine. Opponents thought his Neoplatonism caused him to make the Son inferior to the Father in deity, subordinate in divine essence, an intermediary between the absolute unity or oneness of God and the inferior multiplicity and mutability of the world. Origen overcame this tendency by counterbalancing it with more orthodox affirmations about the Son's full deity. But many of his followers did not maintain Origen's balance. He was also criticized for teaching the preexistence and fall of the soul. Another of his speculations was that in the final restoration, the whole creation, including the devil, would be redeemed. These two teachings were condemned at the Synod of Constantinople (AD 543) and in the Second Council of Constantinople (AD 553, the fifth ecumenical council).

As an exegete of Scripture, Origen is famous for his allegorical interpretations. Most texts, he believed, have a sensible or literal meaning, a moral meaning meant for spiritual progress, and also a spiritual or allegorical one meant for advancing a Christian's knowledge of the God to whom both Testaments bear faithful witness. Only a spiritually discerning and skilled exegete can develop the third sense. To Origen's labors we owe the formation of the *Hexapla*, six versions of the Old Testament arranged in six columns.

Origen's life can be divided into two periods. With a few interruptions, from ca. AD 204 to 230, he taught in Alexandria. In AD

215 or 216, the persecution of Caracalla forced him to flee to Palestine. In AD 218-19 Bishop Demetrius recalled him to Alexandria to resume teaching in the catechetical school. Here he began the most productive period of his career (he produced at least eight hundred works). So that his creativity as a writer might be maximized, secretaries and copyists were placed at his disposal. About AD 230, Origen traveled to the province of Achaia and passed through Caesarea of Palestine. Without Bishop Demetrius's permission, two of Origen's friends ordained him to the priesthood. Consequently, in AD 231 or 232 he was deposed as head of the catechetical school and stripped of his priesthood. Banished from Alexandria, Origen went back to Caesarea, where he began the second major period of his life. During the severe persecution initiated by Emperor Decius (AD 249-51), Origen was thrown into prison (AD 250-51) and tortured. Though he was not killed by his captors, the tortures they inflicted hastened his death.

84

(Origen answers the question, "What is a gospel?")

"Gospel" is either a word that implies the actual presence to the believer of something good or a word that promises the arrival of an expected good. Both of these apply to the books called Gospels. Each gospel is a collection of proclamations that are useful to one who believes and does not misinterpret them. Each gospel brings a benefit and naturally makes the believer glad because it tells of the sojourn of the Firstborn of all creation, Christ Jesus, with humans, on their account and for their salvation. And again, each gospel tells of the sojourn of the good Father in the Son with those of a mind to receive him. By the Gospels a good is proclaimed that had formerly been expected. For to the people, the Messiah was an expected good that the prophets had foretold.

ORIGEN, *COMMENTARY ON THE GOSPEL OF JOHN*, BK. 1, CHAP. 7

MOST LOVING FATHER, whose will it is for us to give thanks for all things, to fear nothing but the loss of you, and to cast all our care on you who care for us: Preserve us from faithless fears and worldly anxieties, that no clouds of this mortal life may hide from us the light of that love that is immortal, and which you have manifested to us in your Son Jesus Christ our Lord; who lives and reigns with you, in the unity of the Holy Spirit, one God, now and forever. Amen.

"EIGHTH SUNDAY AFTER THE EPIPHANY," COLLECTS: CONTEMPORARY, IN BCP

FOR REFLECTION: Matt. 1:18–2:23; Mark 1:39; Luke 4:1-32; John 1:29-51

85

Angels should be named among the evangelists. If among humans there are those who are honored with the ministry of evangelists, and if Jesus himself brings good news and preaches the gospel to the poor, surely those messengers who were made spirits by God, those who are a flame of fire, ministers of the Father, cannot be excluded from the roll of evangelists. An angel standing over the shepherds caused a bright light to shine round about them. He proclaimed, "Fear not; behold I bring you good news of great joy, which shall be to all people; for there is born to you, this day, a Savior, who is Christ the Lord, in the city of David." And having said this, the angels went away from the shepherds into heaven, leaving us to understand how the joy preached to us in the birth of Jesus Christ is glory in the highest to God.

ORIGEN, *COMMENTARY ON THE GOSPEL OF JOHN*, BK. 1, CHAP. 13

SONGS OF PRAISE the angels sang,
Heaven with hallelujahs rang,
When Jehovah's work begun,
When he spoke, and it was done.

Songs of praise awoke the morn,
When the Prince of Peace was born;
Songs of praise arose, when he
Captive led captivity. Amen.

JAMES MONTGOMERY (1771–1854), HYMNARY

FOR REFLECTION: Matt. 1:18-25; **Luke** 1:8-20, 26-38, 46-55; **2:1-18**; Rev. 22:8-9

86

Why should it not be reasonable, seeing that all human enterprises are dependent on faith, to believe God? For who enters on a voyage, contracts a marriage, becomes the father of children, or casts seed into the ground without believing that better things will result from doing so? Belief that better things will follow makes people venture on uncertain enterprises that might not turn out as they hope. If hope and belief in a better future are the support of life in every uncertain human enterprise, why should not belief in God, who is over all things, also be affirmed by Christians? For they believe, on better grounds than one who sails the sea or tills the ground, in the existence of God who is the Creator of all things.

ORIGEN, *AGAINST CELSUS*, BK. 1, CHAP. 11

WE MAY NOT TOUCH YOUR HANDS AND SIDE,
  Nor follow where you trod;
But in your promise we rejoice,
  And cry, "My Lord and God!"

Help then, O Lord, our unbelief;
  And may our faith abound,
To call on you when you are near,
  And seek where you are found:

That, when our life of faith is done,
  In realms of clearer light
We may behold you as you are,
  With full and endless sight. Amen.

HENRY ALFORD (1810-71), HYMNARY

✦✦✦

FOR REFLECTION: Pss. 7:1; 18:1-29; 62:8; Prov. 3:5-26; Isa. 41:10-14; Hab. 3:17-19; Matt. 6:25-34; Luke 12:22-32

87

Christ is the brightness and express image of the divine nature. He came into the world as fully human to sow the seed of his word. All who receive him are brought into union with the Most High God. If we consider Jesus in relation to the deity that was incarnate in him, the things that he did as God incarnate, we see nothing in him that offends our expectations of God, nothing but what is holy. And if we consider his human nature, we see him as distinguished above all others by his intimate communion with God and his absolute wisdom. He suffered as one who was wise and perfect. He suffered for the good of the human race. Not only was his death an example of death endured for the sake of piety, but it was also the first blow in the conflict that will overthrow the power of the devil.

ORIGEN, *AGAINST CELSUS*, BK. 7, CHAP. 17

SOUND ALOUD JEHOVAH'S PRAISES,
Tell abroad his wondrous name;
Heaven the ceaseless anthem raises,
Let the earth her God proclaim:
God, the Hope of every nation,
God, the Source of consolation,
Holy, blessèd Trinity!
This the name from ancient ages
Hidden in its dazzling light;
This the name that kings and sages
Prayed and strove to know aright,
Through God's wondrous incarnation,
Now revealed the world's salvation,
Ever blessèd Trinity! Amen.

HENRY A. MARTIN (1831–1911), HYMNARY

FOR REFLECTION: Mic. 5:2-3; Matt. 1:1-25; Luke 1:26-54; 2:1-40; John 1:14; Rom. 1:3; Col. 2:8-15; 1 John 1:3; 4:2-3

88

We Christians altogether refuse to worship and serve those whom other people worship. We worship with all our power the one God and his only Son, the Word and the Image of God, by prayers and supplications. We offer our petitions to the God of the universe through his only begotten Son. To the Son we first present them and beseech him, as "the propitiation for our sins" and our High Priest, to offer our petitions and sacrifices and prayers to the Most High God. Our faith, therefore, is directed to God through his Son, who strengthens faith in us. We honor the Father when we honor his Son, the Word, Wisdom, Truth, Righteousness, and all that Scripture says of him who is the Son of so great a Father.

ORIGEN, *Against Celsus*, BK. 8, CHAP. 13

THE EARTH, with all that dwell therein,
  With all its wealth untold,
 Belongs to God who founded it
  Upon the seas of old.

. . . .

 Who is this glorious King that comes
  To claim his rightful throne?
 The Lord of Hosts, he is the King
  Of Glory, God alone. Amen.

ATTRIBUTED TO CHARLES JEFFREYS OR L. DEVEREUX (1912), HYMNARY

FOR REFLECTION: Ezra 3:10-13; Pss. 5:7; 24:3-6; Rom. 3:25; 8:26; 1 Cor. 4:15; Eph. 3:11-12; 6:18-19; Phil. 4:6; 1 Thess. 5:17; **1 John 2:2**; 4:10; Rev. 8:3-4

89

(One reason Christians were accused of being atheists was that they had no altars or temples. Origen responds to this issue.)

We Christians believe the spirit of every good person is an altar from which arises truly and spiritually sweet-smelling incense, namely, prayers that ascend to God from a pure conscience. Therefore it is said by John in the Revelation, the prayers of the saints are incense offered to God. And the psalmist said, "Let my prayer come up before you as incense." The statues and gifts that are fit offerings to God do not result from human invention but are created and shaped in us by the Word of God. He also produces in us the virtues by which we imitate "the Firstborn of all creation." Christ has set for us an example of justice, temperance, courage, wisdom, and piety.

ORIGEN, *AGAINST CELSUS*, BK. 8, CHAP. 17

ALMIGHTY GOD, Father of all mercies, we your unworthy servants give you humble thanks for all your goodness and loving-kindness to us and to all whom you have made. We bless you for our creation, preservation, and all the blessings of this life; but above all for your immeasurable love in the redemption of the world by our Lord Jesus Christ; for the means of grace and for the hope of glory. Amen.

"THE GENERAL THANKSGIVING," DAILY EVENING PRAYER: RITE TWO, IN BCP

FOR REFLECTION: 1 Kings 8:22-30; **Pss.** 63:1-2; 66:4-20; **141:2**; Rom. 8:24-27; 12:1-2; Col. 1:18; 3:12-17; Rev. 3:14; 5:8

90

Those who, through the Divine Word, plant and cultivate the virtues that reflect "the Firstborn of all creation" raise statues in worship of Christ their prototype. He is the "the image of the invisible God," God the Only Begotten. Those who put away their old self, corrupt and deluded by lust, and are clothed with the new self, created according to the likeness of God in true righteousness and holiness, take on themselves the very image of him who created them. They raise within themselves a statue such as the Most High God desires.

By contemplating God with a pure heart, Christians become imitators of Christ. The statues they strive to raise are not those of a lifeless and senseless kind. They are not raised to house greedy spirits bent on doing evil things. Instead, Christians are filled with the Spirit of God, who dwells in them. The Spirit takes his abode in those who are being transformed in Christ's image.

ORIGEN, *AGAINST CELSUS*, BK. 8, CHAPS. 17, 18

ALMIGHTY GOD, *Father of all mercies, we pray, give us such an awareness of your mercies, that with truly thankful hearts we may show forth your praise, not only with our lips but in our lives, by giving up ourselves to your service and by walking before you in holiness and righteousness all our days; through Jesus Christ our Lord, to whom, with you and the Holy Spirit, be honor and glory throughout all ages. Amen.*

"THE GENERAL THANKSGIVING," DAILY EVENING PRAYER: RITE TWO, IN BCP

FOR REFLECTION: John 15:1-5; Rom. 5:1–6:14; 8:1-6; 2 Cor. 4:1-7; Eph. 4:22-24

91

(Origen discusses the incarnation of Christ.)

Of Christ it is written, "I do not think that the world could contain the books that might be written" on the glory and majesty of the Son of God. It is impossible to commit to writing all those particulars that belong to the glory of the Savior. After considering questions about the being of the Son of God, we are lost in the deepest amazement that such a nature, preeminent above all others, should have divested itself of its condition of majesty and become human and tabernacled among us, as the grace that was poured upon his lips testifies, as his heavenly Father bore him witness, and as is confessed by the various signs and wonders and miracles that were performed by him.

ORIGEN, *ON FIRST PRINCIPLES*, BK. 2, CHAP. 6, SEC. 1

OF THE FATHER'S LOVE BEGOTTEN,
Ere the worlds began to be,
He the Alpha and Omega,
He the Source, the Ending he,
Of the things that are, that have been,
And that future years shall see,
Evermore and evermore! Amen.

AURELIUS CLEMENS PRUDENTIUS (AD 348–410), TRANS. JOHN M. NEALE (1854) AND HENRY W. BAKER (1859), HYMNARY

FOR REFLECTION: Matt. 11:25-27; 17:1-9; **John** 1:10-17; **21:24-25**; Phil. 2:1-11; Col. 1:15-17; Rev. 5:8-14

92

The Holy Spirit, who cries "Abba Father" in the hearts of the blessed, understands with great sensitivity their sighing in this earthly tabernacle. He "more than intercedes with God in sighs unspeakable." Because of the great love and sympathy he feels for us, he takes on himself our sighs. And by virtue of the wisdom that resides in him, beholding our soul humbled "unto dust" and shut within the body "of humiliation," the Spirit employs no common sighs when he more than intercedes with God for us. With unspeakable sighs that voice the words we cannot speak, the Spirit intercedes for us. And not being content to intercede with God, the Spirit intensifies his intercession to make us "more than conquerors."

Even our understanding cannot pray aright unless the Holy Spirit leads it in prayer. We can no more pray as we should than we can sing a hymn in true harmony with the Spirit, who searches the depths, unless he first sings the hymn in us.

ORIGEN, "INTRODUCTION," *ON PRAYER*, CHAP. 1

> HOLY SPIRIT, *ever working*
> *Through the church's ministry;*
> *Quick'ning, strength'ning, and absolving,*
> *Setting captive sinners free;*
> *Holy Spirit, ever binding*
> *Age to age and soul to soul*
> *In communion never ending,*
> *You we worship and extol. Amen.*

TIMOTHY REES (1874–1939), HYMNARY

✦✦✦

FOR REFLECTION: Matt. 1:18; 3:11-17; 19:28; **Luke** 1:15; **11:1**; 24:29; John 3:5-34; 14:16-26; 15:26; Acts 1:2-16; 2:2-38; 4:8, 31; **Rom.** 1:4; 5:5; **8:15-37**; 1 John 5:6-8

DIONYSIUS OF ALEXANDRIA

No ante-Nicene father ministered during more perilous times than did Bishop Dionysius of Alexandria (ca. AD 190–265). He was called Dionysius the Great because of his learning, his able defense of the Christian faith, and especially the quality of his care for the Christian flock. Dionysius possessed the admirable characteristics of an ecclesiastical leader; he had great executive ability, was of noble character, was kind, and was able to combine great knowledge with devotion to his people.

Born of pagan parents, Dionysius was converted to the Christian faith as an adult. This resulted after extensive reading and reflection. He became one of Origen's outstanding students and later succeeded Heraclas (who became bishop of Alexandria in AD 231 or 232) as head of the catechetical school. Dionysius led the school before being made bishop of Alexandria in AD 248. Then, while serving as bishop, for several years he continued as head of the school.

Dionysius was Greek by birth and expressed Christian doctrine in that language, a fact that sometimes made it difficult for the Latin West to understand him. In fact, the bishop of Rome actually called a synod that condemned Dionysius's teachings, judging that the Alexandrian was saying the Son was created by the Father. Dionysius answered in four books that his accusers had taken his words out of context and had failed to hear his teaching as a whole, where he affirmed the eternality and deity of Father, Son, and Holy Spirit, one God in three distinct persons.

Dionysius's approach to opponents of the Christian faith was to read what they wrote and then try to understand their criticisms before attempting to lead them to faith in Christ. His writings were extensive, but few have survived.

Shortly after Dionysius became bishop, intense persecution of the church erupted in Egypt. It preceded by one year an empire-wide persecution unleashed by Emperor Decius (AD 249-51). The church in Alexandria and throughout Egypt suffered greatly. Many of the clergy as well as laypersons were martyred. Dionysius was able to make his way to exile. From there he led his brutalized flock until Decius's death in 251. During the following brief peace, Dionysius dealt mercifully with the lapsed—those who had received written certificates that proved to the commissioners of sacrifice that a person had regularly worshipped the pagan gods. Possession of a certificate protected a person against further legal proceedings. Then in 258 Emperor Valerian unleashed a merciless persecution. He ordered that bishops, priests, and deacons be executed immediately. Again, Dionysius went into exile. Afterward he openly resumed his episcopal responsibilities until his death on November 17, 265. In addition to the persecution suffered by Christians, during Dionysius's term of service the citizens of Alexandria suffered from civil war, plague, and famine.

93

How shall we respond to those who say all those wise and noble features of the universe are the result of mere chance? I am referring to the individual aspects of nature as well as to the whole system taken collectively. They were declared to be good by God whose command generated their existence. As the Scriptures say, "God saw everything that he had made, and behold, it was very good." But truly, those who deny this do not reflect on the analogies of even small and familiar things they could observe and from which they could learn that no object made with purpose comes into existence by mere chance. Rather, it is created by a skilled workman and is designed to achieve its intended purpose.

DIONYSIUS, *FROM THE BOOKS ON NATURE*, CHAP. 2

IMMORTAL, INVISIBLE, *God only wise,*
In light inaccessible hid from our eyes,
Most blessed, most glorious, the Ancient of Days,
Almighty, victorious, your great name we praise.

. . . .

Life-giving Creator of both great and small,
Of all life the Maker, the true Life of all;
We blossom, then wither like leaves on the tree,
But you are forever, who was and will be.

We worship before you, great Father of light,
While angels adore you, all veiling their sight;
Our praises we render, O Father, to you,
Whom only the splendor of light hides from view. Amen.

WALTER C. SMITH (1824–1908), HYMNARY

✚✚✚

FOR REFLECTION: Gen. 1:31; Neh. 9:6; Job 12:7-9; 38:4-10; Pss. 33:6-9; 136:1-9

94

(Dionysius discusses God's originating and sustaining creativity.)

When a created object falls out of service and becomes useless, it also begins to degrade. Its order dissipates in every casual and unregulated way. This happens because the wisdom and skill by which it was created no longer controls and maintains it. When a house or a city is built, it does not organize its stones as if placed spontaneously on the foundation. One course of stone does not spontaneously place itself on another. Instead, a mason carefully places selected stones in their proper places. If the structure begins to give way, the stones will be separated and scattered about. When a ship is built, the keel does not lay itself. Neither does the mast erect itself in the center, nor do all the other timbers take up their positions accidentally and by their own motion.

DIONYSIUS, *FROM THE BOOKS ON NATURE*, CHAP. 2

> *O LORD, how manifold the works*
> *In wisdom wrought by thee;*
> *The wealth of thy creation fills*
> *The earth and mighty sea.*
>
> . . . .
>
> *My heart shall think upon his grace*
> *In meditation sweet;*
> *My soul, rejoicing in the Lord,*
> *His praises shall repeat. Amen.*

THE PSALTER: WITH RESPONSIVE READINGS (1912), NO. 288, HYMNARY

✦✦✦

FOR REFLECTION: Ps. 146:5-7; Jer. 10:12; 27:5; 31:35-37; 51:15; Acts 17:24-28

95

(Dionysius describes the persecution of Christians in Alexandria that preceded by one year the empire-wide persecution initiated by Emperor Decius [AD 249-51].)

They seized an old man named Metras and commanded him to utter words of impiety; and as he refused, they beat his body with clubs, lacerated his face and eyes with sharp reeds, and then dragged him off to the suburbs and stoned him there. They also seized that most admirable virgin Apollonia, who was then of advanced age. They knocked out all her teeth and cut her jaws. Then, kindling a fire in front of the city, they threatened to burn her alive unless she would join with them to worship the pagan gods. And although she seemed to consider her choice for a little, on being released, she eagerly jumped into the fire and was consumed.

DIONYSIUS, *Epistle to Fabius, Bishop of Antioch*, PARAS. 2-3

BLESSED FEASTS OF BLESSED MARTYRS,
   Holy women, holy men,
With our love and admiration,
   Greet we your return again.
Worthy deeds are theirs, and wonders,
   Worthy of the name they bore;
We, with joyful praise and singing,
   Honor them forevermore. Amen.

UNKNOWN AUTHOR (TWELFTH CENTURY), TRANS. JOHN M. NEALE (1851),
HYMNARY

FOR REFLECTION: Isa. 53:2-10; Matt. 26:3-16; 27:25-44; Luke 22:2-65; Rom. 8:17-37; 2 Cor. 4:8-12; 11:23-27

THE CHURCH IN THE WEST

Jesus charged the apostles to "make disciples of all nations" (Matt. 28:19, NRSV). After Pentecost, they and their associates quickly began to obey Jesus' instructions. Proclamation of the gospel of the kingdom, along with the growth of the church, advanced geographically. The book of Acts tells the story as it involves Jerusalem, Samaria, and the eastern Mediterranean. But the gospel was also spreading elsewhere. The church in Ethiopia traces its beginning to the conversion of an Ethiopian court official under the ministry of Philip the Evangelist (Acts 8:26-39). Tradition is strong that the apostle Thomas preached the good news as far east as India. When in the sixteenth century European priests arrived in southern India to introduce the gospel, they were surprised when told that a more famous missionary, the apostle Thomas, had preceded them.

A beachhead for the gospel in Europe was established during the second missionary journey of the apostle Paul. Accompanied by Silas, Paul proceeded on this mission in response to an invitation that came in a night vision, as recorded in Acts 16:6-15. By this time (ca. AD 49-52), or so it seems, the church in Rome had already been founded. Before AD 58 Paul wrote a letter to this well-established church. One reason for the letter was Paul's desire to use the Roman church as a missionary base for preaching the gospel further west.

For the history of the Western church, Rome occupies a significant position. The most prominent major figures associated with the Roman church before Nicaea (other than Peter and Paul) were Hippolytus (ca. AD 170–ca. 235), who was a student of Irenaeus, and Novatian (ca. AD 200-ca. 258). Both men came into conflict with Roman bishops—Hippolytus over the doctrine of the Trinity, and both men over how to deal with serious postbaptismal sins. As consequences of these conflicts, both men established rival churches. Hippolytus's church enjoyed only a brief life. But the church Novatian founded, though at times sorely persecuted, lasted into the sixth century. Novatian vigorously defended the orthodox faith. However, selections from his extant writings are absent here because they do not lend themselves to devotional reading.

Rome was important. However, for many years the theological center of gravity in the Western church lay elsewhere, namely in North Africa (Carthage and Hippo) and to a lesser extent in Gaul, under the leadership of Irenaeus (d. ca. AD 202). Carthage, which was forcibly integrated into the Roman Empire at the end of the Third Punic War (146 BC), was the home of Tertullian and Cyprian, two figures who towered above the contemporary bishops of Rome. North Africa's prominence would continue in the person of Augustine of Hippo (modern Bizerte, Tunisia). Although Irenaeus was born and reared in the Greek East, wrote in Greek, and hence is not a Latin father, he was identified with the church in Gaul for over fifty years. For that reason, he is included here.

Sadly, the growing differences between the churches in the Latin West and the Greek East would in AD 1054 lead to a formal rupture (the Great Schism) that has yet to be repaired.

Selections in this section will come from Irenaeus, Hippolytus of Rome, Tertullian, and Cyprian.

IRENAEUS

Many early fathers battled doctrinal errors that threatened the church. Given the infancy of the Christian faith and the religious and philosophical ferment that characterized the Greco-Roman world, the threats are not surprising. To no one are we more indebted for a stellar defense of the faith than to Irenaeus of Lyon (d. ca. AD 202), a man who claimed no "display of rhetoric or excellence of composition" (*Against Heresies,* bk. 1, preface) but who will occupy the chair of a doctrinal giant when the banquet of the Lamb commences. He laid solid foundations for subsequent orthodox faith. We know little about his life. He was probably born in one of the maritime provinces of Asia Minor around AD 135. Irenaeus says that as a youth he saw Polycarp of Smyrna (d. 155). Polycarp had been taught by some of the apostles and had conversed with many who had seen Christ (*Against Heresies*, bk. 3, chap. 3, sec. 4).

Around AD 170, Irenaeus went to Celtic Gaul (corresponding roughly to modern-day France and Belgium) and settled in a Christian community in Lyon, center of the Christian mission in Gaul. He became a presbyter (priest) and in AD 177 or 178 was assigned by the clergy of Lyon to deliver a letter to the bishop of Rome on the errors of Montanus (Montanism arose in AD 156 or 157). Many of the clergy in Gaul were suffering imprisonment for their witness (detailed in "The Letter of the Churches of Vienna and Lugdunum [Lyon] to the Churches of Asia and Phrygia" or "Pseud-Irenaeus" [AD 178], in *Remains of the Second and Third Centuries*). While in Rome, Irenaeus encountered other heresies, such as Gnosticism, that seriously threatened the church, a startling realization that prompted him to write *Against Heresies*. On his return home, Irenaeus discovered that Pothinus, the bishop of Lyon, whom Polycarp had sent to establish the Christian mission in Gaul, had been martyred during the persecution ordered by Marcus Aurelius (r. AD 161-80). Irenaeus became the new bishop.

As bishop, he labored as a faithful pastor, as a missionary to the Celts who lived in the area, and as a prolific writer in defense of the faith. We have two of his works and numerous fragments. The first work is *Against Heresies* (*Adversus haereses,* in five books). In this work Irenaeus shows why Gnosticism must never be confused with the Christian faith. He systematically examines and refutes Gnostic myths and exposes how Gnostics erroneously appropriate and integrate Christ and Christian doctrine into their mythological fabrications. Irenaeus also examines other heresies that threatened the church. His second work, *Demonstration (Proof) of the Apostolic Preaching*, was lost until its discovery in 1904. Its purpose is to nurture the faith of Christians.

Irenaeus acted as peacemaker in a potentially disruptive controversy between the bishop of Rome and the churches in Asia Minor over the correct date for celebrating Easter. To him we owe the normalization of the fourfold gospel tradition in the New Testament, a clear and precise statement of the Lord's full humanity, its role in salvation, an explanation of sanctification as *theosis* (becoming godlike), and an unwavering declaration of Christ's deity. Prominent in his teaching is the doctrine that Jesus was so thoroughly human, as well as divine, that he could "recapitulate," or restore, fallen humanity by living in unbroken faithfulness to God. The incarnate Christ did well what Adam did poorly. Irenaeus echoed what the apostle Paul taught in Romans, Ephesians, and other epistles. Irenaeus may have died as a martyr around the year AD 202.

96

The church, though dispersed throughout the whole world, even to the ends of the earth, has received from the apostles and their disciples this faith: She believes in one God, the Father Almighty, Maker of heaven, earth, the sea, and all things that are in them; and in one Christ Jesus, the Son of God, who became incarnate for our salvation; and in the Holy Spirit, who proclaimed through the prophets the dispensations of God, the advent of Christ, his birth by a virgin, his passion, his resurrection from the dead, and his ascension into heaven; and in the humanity of the beloved Christ Jesus, our Lord, and his future manifestation from heaven in the glory of the Father "to gather all things in one" and to raise up anew all flesh of the whole human race in order that to Christ Jesus our Lord and God and Savior and King, by the will of the Father, "every knee should bow, of things in heaven and things in earth and things under the earth and that every tongue should confess" to him and that he should execute just judgment toward all.

IRENAEUS, *AGAINST HERESIES*, BK. 1, CHAP. 10, SEC. 1

GRACIOUS FATHER, we pray for your holy catholic church. Fill it with all truth, in all truth with all peace. Where it is corrupt, purify it; where it is in error, direct it; where in any thing it is amiss, reform it. Where it is right, strengthen it; where it is in want, provide for it; where it is divided, reunite it; for the sake of Jesus Christ your Son our Savior. Amen.

"FOR THE CHURCH," PRAYERS AND THANKSGIVINGS, IN BCP

FOR REFLECTION: Eph. 1:15-23; 4:1-16; **Phil. 2:1-11**; 1 Tim. 3:1-16; Heb. 12:22-23; James 2:1-13

97

(Irenaeus warns against the fictions of the arrogant heretics.)

It is therefore better and more profitable to belong to the simple and unlettered class, and by means of love to attain nearness to God, than by imagining ourselves learned and skillful to be found among those who are blasphemous against God. They conjure up another God in place of God the Father. For this reason Paul said, "Knowledge puffs up, but love edifies." He did not mean to speak against a true knowledge of God, for in that case he would have accused himself, but because he knew that some people, puffed up by a pretence of knowledge, fall away from loving God. They imagine they are perfect. That is why they set forth an imperfect Creator. It is for the purpose of rebuking such pride that Paul said, "Knowledge puffs up." It is therefore better that one should have no knowledge whatsoever of why a single thing in creation exists and still believe in God, and continue in his love, than to be puffed up with false knowledge and fall away from God's love, which is our life. It would be better that we search after no knowledge other than knowledge of Jesus Christ the Son of God, who was crucified for us, than by subtle questions and hairsplitting speculations fall into impiety.

IRENAEUS, *AGAINST HERESIES*, BK. 2, CHAP. 26, SEC. 1

JESUS CALLS US: by your mercies,
Savior, may we hear your call,
Give our hearts to your obedience,
Serve and love you best of all. Amen.

CECIL F. ALEXANDER (1818-95), HYMNARY

FOR REFLECTION: Deut. 13:1-18; Acts 15:24; **1 Cor. 8:1**; 2 Cor. 11:1-4; Gal. 1:6-12; Titus 3:10-11; 2 John vv. 10-11; Jude vv. 3-16

98

(Irenaeus speaks against being consumed by endless speculations.)

The apostle Paul said when other things have passed away, these three, "faith, hope, and love," will endure. For faith, which is directed toward our Master, endures unchanging, assuring us that there is but one true God and that we should truly love him forever, seeing that he alone is our Father. We always hope to be receiving more and more from God and to learn from him because he is good and possesses boundless riches, a kingdom without end, and instruction that can never be exhausted. If, therefore, we leave some questions in the hands of God, we shall preserve our faith uninjured and continue without danger. Then all Scripture, which has been given to us by God, will be found perfectly harmonious. Through the many diversified utterances of Scripture there shall be heard in us one harmonious melody, praising in hymns the God who created all things.

IRENAEUS, *AGAINST HERESIES*, BK. 2, CHAP. 28, SEC. 3

ALMIGHTY GOD, who makes the minds of all faithful people to be of one will; grant to your people that they may love the thing that you command, and desire what you promise, that among the diverse and multiple changes of the world, our hearts may surely there be fixed, where true joys are to be found, through Christ our Lord. Amen.

COLLECT, THE FOURTH SUNDAY AFTER EASTER,
IN THE BOOK OF COMMON PRAYER FOR SCOTLAND (1637)

FOR REFLECTION: Rom. 11:33-36; 14:18-23; **1 Cor. 13:8-13**; 1 Tim. 3:16

99

*(In this reading Irenaeus targets the endless speculations of the Gnostics.
But his words also address Christians in the age of science.)*

We have learned from the Scriptures that God holds supremacy
over all things. But when and how he created the world, neither has Scripture anywhere declared; nor does it become us to
speculate so that by our own opinions we form endless conjec-
tures about God. Let us leave such knowledge in the hands of
God. While we are on the earth, we will "know in part and
prophesy in part." Since, therefore, we know but in part, we
ought to leave all sorts of difficult questions in the hands of him
who bestows his grace on us all.

IRENAEUS, *AGAINST HERESIES*, BK. 2, CHAP. 28, SEC. 7

YOUR WAYS, O LORD, *with wise design,*
Are framed upon your throne above,
And every dark or bending line
Meets in the center of your love.

With feeble light, and half obscure,
Poor mortals your arrangements view,
Not knowing that they all are sure
And, tho' mysterious, just and true.

. . . .

My trusting soul shall meekly learn
To lay her reason at your throne;
Too weak your secrets to discern,
I'll trust you for my guide alone. Amen.

AMBROSE SEARLE (1742–1812), HYMNARY

FOR REFLECTION: Gen. 11:8; Deut. 19:29; Ps. 81; **1 Cor.** 2:10; 12:4-6; **13:9**;
1 Tim. 1:5-7; 6:20-21; 2 Tim. 2:14-21; Titus 3:8-11

100

It is not possible to name the number of gifts that the church, spread throughout the whole world, has received from God in the name of Jesus Christ, who was crucified under Pontius Pilate. These gifts the church administers day by day for the benefit of humankind. She neither practices deception nor takes payment. Freely she has received from God; freely she ministers. Nor does she perform anything by means of angelic invocations, by incantations, or by any other wicked, curious arts. But directing her prayers to the Lord who made all things, in a pure, sincere, and straightforward spirit, and calling on the name of our Lord Jesus Christ, the church has been accustomed to work miracles for the advantage of humankind, and not to lead them into error.

IRENAEUS, *AGAINST HERESIES*, BK. 2, CHAP. 32, SECS. 4-5

LORD, we beseech you to keep your church and household continually in your true religion, that they which do lean only upon hope of your heavenly grace may evermore be defended by your mighty power; through Jesus Christ our Lord. Amen.

COLLECT, THE FIFTH SUNDAY AFTER THE EPIPHANY,
IN THE BOOK OF COMMON PRAYER FOR SCOTLAND (1637)

FOR REFLECTION: Dan. 2:21-23; Matt. 11:28; John 6:27; 16:23-24; 17:22; Acts 8:9, 18; Rom. 5:16-18; 12:6-8; 1 Cor. 12:4-11; Eph. 4:7-8

101

(Irenaeus gives a warning not to stray from the apostles' teaching.)

We have learned from none others the plan of our salvation than from those through whom the gospel has come down to us, which they did at one time proclaim in public and, at a later period, by the will of God, hand down to us in the Scriptures to be the ground and pillar for our faith. After our Lord rose from the dead, the apostles were invested with power from on high when the Holy Spirit came down upon them. They were filled with his gifts and had perfect knowledge of the gospel. They departed to the ends of the earth, preaching the glad tidings of the good things sent from God to us and proclaiming the peace of heaven to humankind.

IRENAEUS, *AGAINST HERESIES*, BK. 3, CHAP. 1, SEC. 1

FOR ALL THE SAINTS, who from their labor rest,
Who you by faith before the world confessed,
Your name, O Jesus, be forever blessed.
Alleluia.

You were their Rock, their Fortress, and their Might,
You, Lord, their Captain in the well-fought fight;
You, in the darkness drear, the Light of light.
Alleluia.

O may your soldiers, faithful, true, and bold,
Fight as the saints who nobly fought of old
And win with them the victor's crown of gold!
Alleluia. Amen.

WILLIAM WALSHAM HOW (1823-97), HYMNARY

✛✛✛

FOR REFLECTION: Matt. 28:16-20; 1 Cor. 3:3-23; 1 Pet. 5:4-11; 2 Pet. 1:15-21; 2 John vv. 5-9; Jude vv. 17-25

102

The apostles taught the Gentiles they should abandon worship of vain blocks of wood and stones, which they imagined to be gods, and worship the true God, who created the whole human family. By means of the creation God nourished, increased, strengthened, and preserved them in being so that they might look for his Son Jesus Christ. With his own blood he redeemed us from apostasy so that we should be a sanctified people. One day he will descend from heaven in his Father's power and pass judgment on all. He will freely give the good things of God to those who shall have kept his commandments. He the Chief Cornerstone, appearing in these last times, has gathered into one and united those that were far off and those that were near.

IRENAEUS, *AGAINST HERESIES*, BK. 3, CHAP. 5, SEC. 3

WHEREFORE I DO ALSO CALL ON YOU, Lord God of Abraham, of Isaac, of Jacob, and of your people Israel, who is the Father of our Lord Jesus Christ, the God who, through the abundance of your mercy, has shown favor toward us, that we should know you, who has made heaven and earth, who rules over all, who is the only and the true God, above whom there is no other God; grant, by our Lord Jesus Christ, the governing power of the Holy Spirit. Give to every reader of this book the opportunity to know you, that you are God alone, to be strengthened in you, and to avoid every heretical, godless, and impious doctrine. Amen.

IRENAEUS, *AGAINST HERESIES*, BK. 3, CHAP. 6, SEC. 4

FOR REFLECTION: Eph. 2:17; Col. 3:1-17; 1 Thess. 4:1-17; 2 Thess. 1:7–2:3

103

The Word, who was in the beginning with God, by whom all things were made, who was also always present with humankind, was in these last days, according to the time appointed by the Father, united to his own workmanship. He became a man liable to suffering. The Son of God did not then begin to exist, being with the Father from the beginning; but when he became incarnate and was made man, he summed up in himself as the second Adam the long line of human beings and furnished us, in a brief, comprehensive manner, with salvation. What we had lost in Adam—namely, to be formed according to the image and likeness of God—that we have recovered in Christ Jesus.

IRENAEUS, *AGAINST HERESIES*, BK. 3, CHAP. 18, SEC. 1

ALMIGHTY GOD, who has given us your only begotten Son to take our nature upon him, and this day to be born of a pure virgin: Grant that we, being regenerate and made your children by adoption and grace, may daily be renewed by your Holy Spirit, through the same our Lord Jesus Christ, who lives and reigns with you and the Holy Spirit, now and forever. Amen.

COLLECT, CHRISTMAS DAY,
IN THE BOOK OF COMMON PRAYER FOR SCOTLAND (1637)

FOR REFLECTION: John 1:1-3; Rom. 1:1-6, 18-32; 5:1-21; 1 Cor. 15:47; Eph. 1:3-14

104

As it was not possible that the man who had once for all been conquered by sin, and who had been destroyed through disobedience, could restore himself and obtain the prize of victory; and as it was also impossible that he who had fallen under the power of sin could attain to salvation—the Son accomplished both these things, being the Word of God, descending from the Father, becoming incarnate, stooping low, even to death, and consummating the arranged plan for our salvation.

IRENAEUS, *AGAINST HERESIES*, BK. 3, CHAP. 18, SEC. 2

ALMIGHTY GOD, who has given your only Son to be to us both a sacrifice for sin and also an example of godly life, give us the grace that we may always most thankfully receive that his inestimable benefit and also daily endeavor to follow the blessed steps of his most holy life through the same Jesus Christ our Lord. Amen.

COLLECT, THE SECOND SUNDAY AFTER EASTER,
IN THE BOOK OF COMMON PRAYER FOR SCOTLAND (1637)

FOR REFLECTION: John 10:7-18; Rom. 10:6-7; 10:9; 14:9; 1 Cor. 1:23; Gal. 3:22-29; Eph. 1:8-12

105

If Christ only appeared to suffer, but did not truly suffer, then when we suffer he will seem to have misled us. He exhorted us to endure suffering and to turn the other cheek. If he only seemed to suffer, we would be above the Master because we do truly suffer. We would sustain what our Master never bore or endured. But as our Lord is alone truly Master, so the Son of God is truly good and patient, the Word of God the Father having truly become the Son of Man. He fought and conquered, for he was man contending for the fathers and through obedience doing away with disobedience completely. He bound the strong man and thereby liberated the weak. He endowed his own handiwork with salvation by destroying sin. For he is a most holy and merciful Lord and loves the human race.

IRENAEUS, *AGAINST HERESIES*, BK. 3, CHAP. 18, SEC. 6

O GOD ALMIGHTY, grant to us the fountain of regeneration and the garment of incorruption, which is the true life. Deliver us from all ungodliness, give no place to the adversary against us, and cleanse us from all filthiness of flesh and spirit. Dwell in us by your Christ, bless our goings out and our comings in, and order our affairs for our good and your glory. Make us to be partakers of your divine mysteries through Christ who is our hope, who died for us, by whom glory and worship be given to you in the Holy Spirit forever. Amen.

CLEMENTINE LITURGY (LATE FOURTH CENTURY),
IN *CONSTITUTIONS OF THE HOLY APOSTLES*, BK. 8, SEC. 2.6

FOR REFLECTION: Matt. 5:13, 39; 12:29; 26:45; 27:45-50; Mark 15:34; Phil. 2:7; Heb. 2:9; 4:15; 12:2-3; 1 Pet. 1:11; 2:21-23

106

(Irenaeus shows the necessity of Christ's full humanity and full deity.)

The most holy and merciful Lord caused human nature to cleave to and to become one with God. Unless as a man the Word incarnate had overcome the enemy of man, the enemy would not have been legitimately vanquished. And unless it had been God who had freely given salvation, we could never have securely possessed it. And unless we humans had been joined to God, we could never have become partakers of incorruptibility. For it was incumbent on the Mediator between God and humanity, by his relationship to both, to bring both God and man to friendship and concord. Christ presented man to God and revealed God to man. For how could we have been adopted as children of God unless we had received from him, through the Son, that fellowship that joins us to God? This could not have happened unless God's Word, having been made flesh, had entered into communion with us.

IRENAEUS, *AGAINST HERESIES*, BK. 3, CHAP. 18, SEC. 7

O THAT BIRTH FOREVER BLESSED,
　When the Virgin, full of grace,
By the Holy Spirit conceiving,
　Bore the Savior of our race,
And the Babe, the world's Redeemer,
　First revealed his sacred face,
Evermore and evermore! Amen.

AURELIUS CLEMENS PRUDENTIUS (AD 348–410), TRANS. JOHN M. NEALE (1854) AND HENRY W. BAKER (1859), HYMNARY

FOR REFLECTION: Deut. 32:4; Rom. 5:11-19; Eph. 1:3-12; Phil. 2:6-8

107

It behooved him who was to destroy sin and redeem human-kind from the power of death that he should himself be made that very same thing, namely, man, who had been drawn by sin into bondage and was held captive by death. Sin had to be destroyed by man (the incarnate Christ) so that humankind could be freed from death. As by the disobedience of the one man who was originally molded from virgin soil, the many were made sinners and forfeited life, so it was necessary that by the obedience of one man who was originally born from a virgin, many should be justified and receive salvation. Thus, the Word of God was made man. If he falsely appeared to be human, then his work was not true. But what he appeared to be, that he was. God recapitulated in himself the ancient formation of man, that he might destroy sin, deprive death of its power, and give life to humankind. Therefore his works are true.

IRENAEUS, *AGAINST HERESIES*, BK. 3, CHAP. 18, SEC. 7

NOW TO HIM who is able to bring us all into his everlasting kingdom by his grace and goodness, through his only begotten Son Jesus Christ, to him be glory, honor, power, and majesty, forever. Amen.

THE *MARTYRDOM OF POLYCARP*, CHAP. 20

FOR REFLECTION: Matt. 20:22; 26:39; Mark 10:38; Rom. 5:19; Heb. 2:4—3:1

108

True knowledge, then, consists in the understanding of Christ, which Paul terms the wisdom of God hidden in a mystery, which "the natural man does not receive." It is the doctrine of the cross, which if any person "taste," he or she will reject the disputations and quibbles of those proud and puffed-up people who dabble in matters about which they have no understanding. The wisdom of God is not secretive: "The word is near you, in your mouth and in your heart." The wisdom of God is easy to comprehend for all those who will be obedient.

IRENAEUS, *FRAGMENTS FROM THE LOST WRITINGS OF IRENAEUS*, NO. 36

GOD, the strength of all them that trust in you, mercifully accept our prayers; and because the weakness of our mortal nature can do no good thing without you, grant us the help of your grace, that in keeping your commandments, we may please you both in will and deed; through Jesus Christ our Lord. Amen.

COLLECT, THE FIRST SUNDAY AFTER TRINITY, IN THE BOOK OF COMMON PRAYER FOR SCOTLAND (1637)

FOR REFLECTION: Deut. 30:14; Rom. 10:1-17; 1 Cor. 2:14; Col. 2:18; 1 Tim. 6:4-5; 1 Pet. 2:3

109

The wisdom of God will make us like Christ if we experience "the power of his resurrection and the fellowship of his sufferings." For this is the heart of the apostles' teaching and the most holy "faith delivered to us," which even the unlearned can receive and which those of slight learning have taught to others. We do not give "heed to endless genealogies" but study rather to observe a straightforward course of life; lest, having been deprived of the Divine Spirit, we fail to attain to the kingdom of heaven. Truly the first thing is to deny oneself and to follow Christ. Those who do this are borne onward to perfection, having fulfilled their Teacher's will. They become children of God by spiritual regeneration and heirs of the kingdom of heaven. Those who seek the kingdom of heaven will never be forsaken.

IRENAEUS, *FRAGMENTS FROM THE LOST WRITINGS OF IRENAEUS*, NO. 36

COME, THOU HOLY SPIRIT, come!
And from thy celestial home
  Shed a ray of light divine!
Come, thou Father of the poor!
Come, thou Source of all our store!
  Come, within our bosoms shine! Amen.

UNKNOWN AUTHOR (TWELFTH CENTURY AD),
TRANS. EDWARD CASWALL (1849), HYMNARY

FOR REFLECTION: 1 Cor. 1:11-31; **Phil. 3:6-16; 1 Tim. 1:4**; Heb. 2:1-3; **Jude v. 3**

110

Those who are acquainted with the teachings of the apostles know that the Lord instituted a new oblation (offering) in the new covenant. John declares in the Apocalypse: "The incense is the prayers of the saints." Paul exhorts us "to present our bodies a living sacrifice, holy, acceptable to God, which is your reasonable service." And again, "Let us offer the sacrifice of praise, that is, the fruit of the lips." These new oblations are not according to the law; they are according to the Spirit, for we must worship God "in spirit and in truth."

IRENAEUS, *FRAGMENTS FROM THE LOST WRITINGS OF IRENAEUS*, NO. 37

O GOD OF TRUTH, O Lord of might,
Who, ordering time and change aright,
Sendest the early morning ray,
Kindling the glow of perfect day;

Extinguish thou each sinful fire,
And banish every ill desire;
And keeping all the body whole,
Shed forth thy peace upon the soul.

O Father, that we ask be done,
Through Jesus Christ, thine only Son;
Who, with the Holy Spirit and thee,
Shall live and reign eternally. Amen.

AMBROSE (AD 340-97), TRANS. JOHN M. NEALE (1852), HYMNARY

FOR REFLECTION: John 4:19-26; Rom. 12:1-2; Heb. 13:7-16; Rev. 5:8-10

111

The Scriptures acknowledge with regard to Christ that just as he is the Son of Man, so he is not merely a man; as he is flesh, so he is also spirit and the Word of God and God. And as he was born of Mary in the last times, so did he also eternally proceed from God as the First Begotten of every creature; and as he hungered, so did he satisfy others; and as he thirsted, so did he of old cause the Jews to drink, for the "Rock was Christ" himself. Jesus now gives to his believing people power to drink the spiritual waters that spring up to life eternal.

IRENAEUS, *FRAGMENTS FROM THE LOST WRITINGS OF IRENAEUS*, NO. 52

MAKER, in whom we live, in whom we are and move,
The glory, power, and praise receive for your creating love.
Let all the angel throng give thanks to God on high,
While earth repeats the joyful song and echoes to the sky.

Incarnate Deity, let all the ransomed race
Render in thanks their lives to you for your redeeming grace.
The grace to sinners showed you heavenly choirs proclaim,
And cry, "Salvation to our God, salvation to the Lamb!"

Spirit of Holiness, let all your saints adore
Your sacred energy and bless your heart-renewing power.
No angel tongues can tell your love's ecstatic height,
The glorious joy unspeakable, the beatific sight. Amen.

CHARLES WESLEY (1707-88), HYMNARY

FOR REFLECTION: John 4:14; 8:52-59; 20:22; **1 Cor. 10:4**; 2 Cor. 13:4; Eph. 4:9-10; 1 John 1:1-2; **Rev.** 1:8-18; 5:13-14; **7:10**

112

The Law and the Prophets and the Gospels have declared that Christ was born of a virgin and suffered on the cross, was raised also from the dead, and taken up to heaven; that he was glorified and reigns forever. He is the Man among men, Son in the Father, God in God, King to all eternity. He was sold with Joseph, and he guided Abraham; he was bound along with Isaac and wandered with Jacob; with Moses he was Leader and, respecting the people, Legislator. He preached in the prophets, was incarnate of a virgin, born in Bethlehem, and received by John and baptized in the Jordan; he was tempted in the desert and proved to be the Lord. He gathered the apostles together and preached the kingdom of heaven, gave light to the blind and raised the dead, was seen in the temple, but was not held by the people as worthy of credit; he was arrested by the priests, conducted before Herod, and condemned in the presence of Pilate; he manifested himself in the body, was suspended on a beam of wood, and was raised from the dead; he was shown to the apostles and, having been carried up to heaven, sits at the right hand of the Father and has been glorified by him as the Resurrection of the dead—he is Jesus Christ our Savior.

IRENAEUS, *FRAGMENTS FROM THE LOST WRITINGS OF IRENAEUS*, NO. 54

ALMIGHTY GOD, you have poured upon us the new light of your incarnate Word: Grant that this light, enkindled in our hearts, may shine forth in our lives; through Jesus Christ our Lord, who lives and reigns with you, in the unity of the Holy Spirit, one God, now and forever. Amen.

"FIRST SUNDAY AFTER CHRISTMAS," COLLECTS: CONTEMPORARY, IN BCP

FOR REFLECTION: Matt. 1:18-23; Luke 1:26-38; 4:1-13; John 8:12; 12:46-50; 20:1-31; 1 Cor. 10:1-4; 1 Tim. 2:3-6; Titus 3:3-7

113

During the growth process, no one expects maturity or full development of the premature grape or fig. Anyone can see that the fruit, though partly ripe, is still somewhat imperfect. The vinedresser does not for that reason despise the immature grape as worthless. He just gathers it with pleasure as having appeared early in the season. Nor does he consider whether the early grape possesses perfect sweetness. Nay, he at once experiences satisfaction from the thought that this grape has appeared before the rest. In the same way, when God sees the faithful possessing wisdom, even though imperfect, and having but a small degree of faith, overlooks their defects; he does not reject them. Nay, on the contrary, he kindly welcomes and accepts them as premature fruit and honors the faithful as marked by virtue. He makes allowance for the imperfection, as being among the wine that flows from the grapes before the mature harvest is pressed. He highly esteems the imperfect fruit.

IRENAEUS, *FRAGMENTS FROM THE LOST WRITINGS OF IRENAEUS*, NO. 55

O GOD, who wonderfully created, and yet more wonderfully restored, the dignity of human nature: Grant that we may share the divine life of him who humbled himself to share our humanity, your Son Jesus Christ; who lives and reigns with you, in the unity of the Holy Spirit, one God, forever and ever. Amen.

"SECOND SUNDAY AFTER CHRISTMAS DAY,"
COLLECTS: CONTEMPORARY, IN BCP

FOR REFLECTION: Matt. 5:13-16, 45; 6:9-15; Luke 12:31-32; John 15:1-16; Rom. 14:3-4, 17-23

114

(Irenaeus discusses the Trinitarian character of salvation.)

Regeneration proceeds through these three points: God the Father bestows on us regeneration through his Son by the Holy Spirit. For as many as are led by the Spirit of God are led to the Word, that is, to the Son; and the Son brings them to the Father; and the Father causes them to possess incorruption. Without the Spirit it is not possible to behold the Word of God, nor without the Son can anyone draw near to the Father. For the knowledge of the Father is the Son, and the knowledge of the Son of God comes through the Holy Spirit; and according to the good pleasure of the Father, the Son ministers and dispenses the Spirit to whomsoever the Father wills and as he wills.

IRENAEUS, *THE DEMONSTRATION OF THE APOSTOLIC PREACHING*, PARA. 5

ALMIGHTY AND EVERLASTING GOD, you have given to us your servants grace, by the confession of a true faith, to acknowledge the glory of the eternal Trinity, and in the power of your divine Majesty to worship the Unity: Keep us steadfast in this faith and worship, and bring us at last to see you in your one and eternal glory, O Father; who with the Son and the Holy Spirit lives and reigns, one God, forever and ever. Amen.

"FIRST SUNDAY AFTER PENTECOST: TRINITY SUNDAY," COLLECTS: CONTEMPORARY, IN BCP

FOR REFLECTION: Matt. 12:28; 28:19; Luke 1:25; 3:22; John 1:32; 14:16-26; Acts 1:2-5; 2 Cor. 1:21-22; 3:17; 13:14; Gal. 4:4-5

115

God the Father was very merciful. He sent his creative Word, who in coming to deliver us came to the very place and spot where we had died. He broke our fetters. His light appeared and made the darkness of our prison disappear. He hallowed our birth and destroyed death. He manifested our resurrection by becoming the Firstborn of the dead. He raised the fallen and lifted us to heaven, to the right hand of the glory of the Father.

IRENAEUS, *THE DEMONSTRATION OF THE APOSTOLIC PREACHING*, PARA. 38

O GOD, whose blessed Son came into the world that he might destroy the works of the devil and make us children of God and heirs of eternal life: Grant that, having this hope, we may purify ourselves as he is pure; that, when he comes again with power and great glory, we may be made like him in his eternal and glorious kingdom; where he lives and reigns with you and the Holy Spirit, one God, forever and ever. Amen.

"PROPER 27," COLLECTS: CONTEMPORARY, IN BCP

FOR REFLECTION: Phil. 2:5-10; Heb. 4:14-16; 5:5-10; 10:7-23; James 5:11; 2 Pet. 3:9, 15

116

(Irenaeus discusses the apostles and their message.)

After receiving the power of the Holy Spirit, the apostles were sent forth by Christ into all the world. They effected the calling of the Gentiles and showed humankind the way of life. They turned people from idols, fornication, and covetousness, cleansing their souls and bodies by the baptism of water and the Holy Spirit. They imparted the Holy Spirit to all who believed; thus they ordered and established the churches. By faith, love, and hope they established that which was foretold by the prophets—the calling of the Gentiles—according to the mercy of God that was extended to them. Through their ministry they brought the gospel to light. The Gentiles were admitted to the promise made to the fathers, namely, that those who would believe in and love the Lord, and who would continue in holiness, righteousness, and patient endurance, God of all would grant eternal life by the resurrection of the dead through him who died and rose again, Jesus Christ. To him the Father has delivered rule over all existing things, the living and dead, and also the judgment.

IRENAEUS, *THE DEMONSTRATION OF THE APOSTOLIC PREACHING*, PARA. 41

Almighty God, you have built your church on the foundation of the apostles and prophets, Jesus Christ himself being the Chief Cornerstone: Grant us so to be joined together in unity of spirit by their teaching, that we may be made a holy temple acceptable to you; through Jesus Christ our Lord, who lives and reigns with you and the Holy Spirit, one God, forever and ever. Amen.

"PROPER 8," COLLECTS: CONTEMPORARY, IN BCP

FOR REFLECTION: Rom. 9:1–10:13; 1 Cor. 4:9-13; 2 Cor. 12:12; Eph. 2:13-22; 2 Pet. 1:2-21

HIPPOLYTUS OF ROME

Information about Hippolytus is laced with blank spaces at critical points. He was probably born sometime between AD 170 and 175. We know that around AD 212 he was present in Rome as a presbyter (priest). He referred to himself as a disciple of Irenaeus. It is not clear whether this means he actually studied under Irenaeus or became his student by reading his works.

The character and extent of Hippolytus's writings reveal a talented and well-educated person. Approximately thirty-five works are attributed to him, some of which are extant. Although Hippolytus lived in Rome, like Irenaeus, he wrote in Greek at a time when Latin was replacing Greek as the language of the church in Rome. His *Refutation of All Heresies* (ten books) demonstrates a well-developed familiarity with the Greek philosophers and the heresies that had beset the church prior to his time. Like his teacher, Hippolytus was certain philosophy was the mother of heresy.

Hippolytus exhibits strong reliance on the Scriptures for the formation of theology and for refuting heresies. Distortions of Christian doctrine would not have arisen, Hippolytus says, if those responsible for them had demonstrated fidelity to the whole of Scripture, not to carefully chosen portions that support their aberrant doctrines. His counsel on this score has stood the test of time and calls for our attention today. His unwavering commitment to sound exegesis, his expertise as an apologist for the faith, his joining of piety with moral discipline, and his zeal for orthodox doctrine are main reasons Hippolytus was and continues to be a revered father of the church. An interesting example of Hippolytus's eminence is that when Origen visited Rome in AD 212, he went to listen to Hippolytus's lecture.

Hippolytus ran afoul of Zephyrinus, the bishop of Rome, and his successor Callistus. The reasons were probably personal as well as doctrinal. They disagreed sharply over the doctrine of the Trinity and the forgiveness of serious postbaptismal sins. When in AD 117 Callistus became bishop, Hippolytus refused to recognize him. This decision led to a formal rupture. Hippolytus did not go quietly; he set up his own church and became its bishop. Rival bishops of Rome, or popes, are called antipopes. Rivalry between the two churches continued for eighteen years. In AD 235 Emperor Maximinus Thrax instigated a persecution of Christians and did not distinguish between rival bishops and churches. He ordered the seizure and deportation of Hippolytus and Pontianus—Callistus's successor—to Sardinia, where both of them soon perished (AD 235), reportedly as martyrs. Before his death, Hippolytus made peace with Pontianus and the Roman church. He urged members of his church to embrace his reconciliation with Rome. After the deaths of Pontianus and Hippolytus, their bodies were returned to Rome for burial. Unlike Novatian, Hippolytus died in restored fellowship with the Roman church. Consequently, the Roman Catholic Church reveres Hippolytus as a saint and martyr. In 1551 a marble statue of Hippolytus seated in a chair was discovered in Rome near the ancient Church of St. Lawrence.

117

*(Discussing the source of heresies, Hippolytus
provides ageless counsel for the church.)*

Whenever heretics attempt to undermine the Christian faith, they first mutilate the Scriptures. If they would treat the Scriptures as a whole, they would not err in understanding why the Bible was written. There is, brethren, one God, the knowledge of whom we gain from the Holy Scriptures and from no other source. For just as a person who wants to be skilled in the wisdom of this world will be unable to obtain it unless that person first masters the teaching of the philosophers, so all of us who wish to practice Christian piety will be unable to learn its practice from any other source than the oracles of God. Whatever things, then, the Holy Scriptures declare, these let us study, and whatsoever things they teach, these let us embrace; and what the Father wants us to believe, let us believe; and as he wills the Son to be glorified, let us glorify him; and as he wills the Holy Spirit to be bestowed, let us receive him.

HIPPOLYTUS, *AGAINST THE HERESY OF ONE NOETUS*, PARAS. 4, 9

O CHRIST, THE WORD INCARNATE,
   O Wisdom from on high,
O Truth, unchanged, unchanging,
   O Light of our dark sky!
We praise thee for the radiance
   That from the Scripture's page,
A lantern to our footsteps,
   Shines on from age to age. Amen.

WILLIAM WALSHAM HOW (1823-97), HYMNARY

FOR REFLECTION: John 16:13-15; 17:1-8; Rom. 10:9-13; 15:1-9; 16:24-27; 1 Cor. 15:1-8; Gal. 3:8-14; 1 Pet. 4:16; Rev. 15:1-4

118

Let us therefore believe, dear brethren, according to the tradition of the apostles. God the Word came down from heaven and entered into the holy Virgin Mary. Taking the flesh from her, assuming also a human, rational soul, and becoming all that man is with the exception of sin, he redeems fallen humanity and confers immortality on all who believe on his name. In all, therefore, the word of truth is demonstrated to us, namely, that the Father is One, whose Word is present with him by whom he made all things, whom also the Father sent forth in later times for the salvation of humankind. This Word was preached by the Law and the Prophets as being elected to come incarnate into the world. Even as he was preached, even so did he come and manifest himself, being by the Virgin and the Holy Spirit made the new humanity. In that he had the divine nature of the Father, and taking to himself humanity through the Virgin, he came forth into the world, revealed as God in perfect human form. For it was not in mere appearance, but in truth he became man.

HIPPOLYTUS, *AGAINST THE HERESY OF ONE NOETUS*, PARA. 17

O GOD, who through your great and unspeakable love did condescend to the weakness of us your servants, and has in the gospel given us eternal life, preserve us in the sanctification of your Holy Spirit. Being made holy, let us receive participation and inheritance with all your saints that have been well-pleasing to you since the world began. We live in the light of your countenance, through the mercy of your only begotten Son, our Lord and God and Savior Jesus Christ. With him you are blessed, together with your all-holy, good, and quickening Spirit. Blessed and glorified is your all-precious and glorious name, Father, Son, and Holy Spirit, now and to all eternity. Amen.

THE DIVINE LITURGY OF JAMES THE HOLY APOSTLE (CA. AD 150–200)

FOR REFLECTION: 1 Thess. 5:1-11; 2 Tim. 2:1-7; James 4:7-8; 1 John 5:1-5; Jude vv. 3-4

119

Although he is revealed to be God incarnate, Jesus Christ does not refuse the conditions of human existence. He hungers, toils, and thirsts in weariness. He flees those who want to kill him and prays when in trouble. He who as God has a sleepless nature nevertheless slumbers on a pillow. And he who came into the world to suffer nevertheless prays to have the cup of suffering pass from him. He who strengthens those who believe on him nevertheless sweats blood in agony. And he who knew what manner of person Judas was nevertheless is betrayed by him. And he who will himself judge the whole earth nevertheless was judged by Caiaphas, counted as nothing by Herod, and scourged by Pilate. And he at whose beckoning stand thousands of thousands and myriads of myriads of angels and archangels nevertheless was mocked by Roman soldiers. And he who created the heavens is yet fastened to a wooden cross. And he who said, "I have power to lay down my life, and I have power to take it again," nevertheless bows his head and gives up the ghost. And he who bountifully gives life to all nevertheless has his side pierced with a spear. And he who raises the dead nevertheless is wrapped in linen and laid in a tomb. And he, though himself the Resurrection and the Life, on the third day is raised by the Father.

HIPPOLYTUS, *AGAINST THE HERESY OF ONE NOETUS*, PARA. 18

O LOVING WISDOM OF OUR GOD!
When all was sin and shame,
A second Adam to the fight
And to the rescue came. Amen.

JOHN HENRY NEWMAN (1801-90), HYMNARY

FOR REFLECTION: Isa. 53:4; Matt. 17:5; 27:29; Luke 23:44-46; **John 10:18;** 11:51-52; 19:23-24, 28-37

120

All these things Christ has finished for us, who for our sakes became just as we are. For he has "borne our infirmities and carried our diseases; and for our sakes he was afflicted." This is he who was hymned by the angels, seen by the shepherds, waited for by Simeon, and witnessed to by Anna. This is he who was inquired after by the wise men and indicated by the star; he was engaged in his Father's house, was pointed to by John the Baptist, and witnessed to by the Father from above in the voice, "This is my beloved Son; hear him." He is crowned victor over the devil. This is Jesus of Nazareth. For his sake the sun is darkened, the day has no light, the rocks are shattered, the veil is rent, the foundations of the earth are shaken, the graves are opened, the dead are raised, and the rulers are ashamed when they see the Director of the universe on the cross, closing his eyes and giving up the ghost. Creation shrouded itself in darkness. This is he who is set down on the right hand of the Father, who will come again as the Judge of the living and the dead. This is the God who for our sakes became man, to whom also the Father has put all things in subjection.

HIPPOLYTUS, *AGAINST THE HERESY OF ONE NOETUS*, PARA. 18

O LOVE, how deep, how broad, how high,
How passing thought and fantasy,
That God, the Son of God, should take
Our mortal form for mortals' sake! Amen.

ATTRIBUTED TO THOMAS À KEMPIS (FIFTEENTH CENTURY),
TRANS. BENJAMIN WEBB (1854), HYMNARY

FOR REFLECTION: Isa. 53:4; **Matt. 17:5**; 27:39-54; Acts 5:31; 7:55-56; Eph. 1:17-21; Col. 3:1-5; Heb. 12:1-3; 1 Pet. 3:21-22

TERTULLIAN

Tertullian (ca. AD 160-ca. 225), called the Father of Latin Theology, is recognized as one of the most doctrinally original fathers. He was born in Carthage. At about age forty, Tertullian became a Christian while living in Rome, where he was educated and might have practiced law. After returning to Carthage, Tertullian initiated a prodigious literary defense and exposition of Christian doctrine and practice that date from about AD 190 to 220. Of his existing works, there are thirty-one; at least fifteen works are lost.

Tertullian was one of the most theologically productive early fathers. Some of his teachings the church either subsequently rejected or refined. The church never accepted his belief that the souls of all persons were originally contained in Adam. But we continue to be indebted to Tertullian for his explanation of the Trinity and Christology. He defined the Trinity as three distinct persons who share one divine substance (three persons, one substance). The Father is God, the Son is God, and the Holy Spirit is God, One God. In his defense of the Scriptures, Tertullian told heretics that because they had departed from the faith, they had lost their right to appeal to the Scriptures. Unlike some fathers who believed some of the philosophers had achieved valuable theological insights, Tertullian severely discounted any positive relationship between philosophy and the Christian faith. He famously asked in *The Prescription against Heretics*, "What indeed has Athens to do with Jerusalem?" (chap. 7). Tertullian strongly influenced Bishop Cyprian of Carthage and other Christian teachers.

Knowing how to evaluate Tertullian has always been a challenge for the church. For years he taught and wrote under the good graces of the church catholic. Working in Carthage, he ably defended the Christian faith and the church against its persecutors and heretics. But around the year AD 207 Tertullian moved in a different direction by joining the Montanists, founded by Montanus.

Possibly a former pagan priest, Montanus became a Christian and was baptized around AD 155. Shortly thereafter he declared himself possessed by the Holy Spirit. He began to prophesy and was soon joined by two prophetesses, Priscilla and Maximilla. They proclaimed that a new dispensation, the dispensation of the Holy Spirit, had been revealed to them. This was God's final revelation. The new age of the Spirit surpassed, but did not contradict, what had been revealed in the New Testament. The Montanists believed the faith of Christians had grown cold and the church had sorely relaxed its moral discipline. Their teaching also included novel elements of eschatology; they taught that the end of the world was soon to come and that the New Jerusalem would be established in the town of Pepuza in Phrygia (today's Turkish district of Karahallı).

Why did Tertullian become a Montanist? The reasons are not clear. No doubt he was attracted by their moral rigor and their protest against the ease with which the church often forgave Christians who sinned openly, and he also believed the church was becoming more interested in hierarchical power than in the manifestation of the Holy Spirit. Whatever his reasons, Tertullian never compromised his commitment to orthodox doctrine. He remains a major and revered father of the church.

Some of Tertullian's works were written before he became a Montanist, and some afterward. In his *Apology* (AD 197), addressed to the rulers of the Roman Empire, Tertullian defends the Christian faith against pagan detractors. In numerous works he attacks various heresies, including the teaching of Marcion, who held that the Old and New Testaments represent two irreconcilable "Gods." *To the Gentiles* and *On the Testimony of the Soul* tell about the persecutions and how the Christians responded. *To the Martyrs* consoles and exhorts imprisoned Christians facing martyrdom by exposure to the lions and extols their heroism as soldiers of Christ. Tertullian produced numerous works that address practical concerns and that teach Christians how to live godly lives in a pagan world.

121

(The early Christian "love feast" or "agape meal" was distinct from the Eucharist but closely associated with it.)

Just as our love feast commenced with prayer, so with prayer it closes. We go from it, not like troops of mischief-doers, nor bands of vagabonds, nor to break out into licentious acts, but to have as much care for our modesty and chastity as if we had been at a school of virtue rather than a feast. Let our love feast be condemned if any complaint can be justly laid against it. But who has ever suffered harm from our assemblies? We are in our congregations just what we are when separated from each other; we are as a community what we are as individuals. We injure no one; we trouble nobody. When the upright, when the virtuous, meet together, when the pious, when the pure, assemble in congregation, you ought not to call that a seditious faction, but a *curia*, namely, the court of God.

TERTULLIAN, *APOLOGY*, CHAP. 39

ALMIGHTY GOD, you have given us grace at this time with one accord to make our common supplication to you; and you have promised through your well-beloved Son that when two or three are gathered together in his name, you will be in the midst of them: Fulfill now, O Lord, our desires and petitions as may be best for us; granting us in this world knowledge of your truth, and in the age to come life everlasting. Amen.

"A PRAYER OF ST. CHRYSOSTOM," DAILY EVENING PRAYER: RITE TWO, IN BCP

FOR REFLECTION: Acts 2:46; Rom. 12:3-21; 1 Cor. 12:12-31; Eph. 5:25—6:17

122

The principal crime of the human race, the highest guilt charged upon the world, the primary fault that has brought judgment, is idolatry. For although each fault retains its own distinct feature, although it is destined to judgment under its own proper name, yet it is identified under the *general* account of idolatry. Set aside names; examine individual deeds; the idolater is also a murderer. In idolatry all crimes are present, and in all crimes idolatry is present. This is because all faults stem from opposition to God. And there is nothing that tastes of opposition to God that is not attributed to demons and unclean spirits, whose property idols are.

TERTULLIAN, *ON IDOLATRY*, CHAP. 1

Holy Spirit, Light divine,
Shine upon this heart of mine;
Chase the shades of night away;
Turn the darkness into day.

. . . .

Holy Spirit, all divine,
Dwell within this heart of mine;
Cast down every idol throne,
Reign supreme, and reign alone. Amen.

ANDREW REED (1787–1862), HYMNARY

FOR REFLECTION: Exod. 20:3-6; Isa. 44:9-20; Jer. 7:21-28; 2 Cor. 10:17; Gal. 5:19-21; Col. 3:5; 1 John 5:21

123

Idolatry has many branches; it diffuses through many veins. We must diligently guard against its expansion. Idolatry can subvert the servants of God in many ways, not only when it is open but also when it comes disguised. Most people recognize idolatry only when it is openly practiced, such as when a person burns incense to an idol, sacrifices an animal, gives a sacrificial banquet, or is bound to some sacred pagan function or priesthood. The devil's ingenuity in malice, and the Lord's discipline by which he fortifies us, would garner restricted range if idolatry were limited only to its open manifestations. Our righteousness will not transcend that of the scribes and Pharisees unless we recognize the many ways idolatry can be practiced. The fountain of all unrighteousness is idolatry. We must be fortified against its many manifestations, not just against its flagrant manifestations.

TERTULLIAN, *ON IDOLATRY*, CHAP. 2

O LORD GOD ALMIGHTY, the Father of your Christ, your blessed Son, you who separated us from the communion of the ungodly, unite us with those that are consecrated to you in holiness; confirm us in the truth by the assistance of your Holy Spirit; reveal to us what things we are ignorant of, supply what things we are defective in, and confirm us in what things we already know. Bless those that bow before you. Grant them the petitions of their hearts that are for their good. And do not reject any one of them from your kingdom; but sanctify, and assist them; deliver them from the adversary and every enemy; keep their houses and guard "their comings in and their goings out." For to you belong the glory, praise, and adoration and to your Son Jesus, your Christ, our Lord and God and King, and to the Holy Ghost, forever and ever. Amen.

CONSTITUTIONS OF THE HOLY APOSTLES LITURGY (LATE FOURTH CENTURY), IN
CONSTITUTIONS OF THE HOLY APOSTLES, BK. 8, SEC. 2.15

FOR REFLECTION: Deut. 12:32–13:18; **Ps. 121:8**; Hos. 11:1-4; Rom. 1:18-32; Rev. 9:20

124

Amid the many reefs and inlets, amid the many shallows and straits of idolatry, Faith, her sails filled by the Spirit of God, safely navigates. She is safe, if cautious; she is secure, if intently watchful. Those who are washed overboard by idolatry will drown. They will be swallowed by a whirlpool. Their ship will run aground and be wrecked. The waves of idolatry will suffocate; its eddies will draw a person down to death. Let no Christian say, "Who can be this careful? He would first have to leave the world." Nothing can be easier than to guard against idolatry if our fear of it is our strongest fear. Any effort to guard against idolatry is negligible when compared to its threat.

TERTULLIAN, ON IDOLATRY, CHAP. 24

A CHARGE TO KEEP I HAVE,
A God to glorify!
A never-dying soul to save,
And fit it for the sky;

. . . .

Arm me with jealous care,
As in your sight to live;
And, O your servant, Lord, prepare
A strict account to give.

Help me to watch and pray,
And on yourself rely;
Assured, if I my trust betray,
I shall forever die. Amen.

CHARLES WESLEY (1708-88), HYMNARY

✝✝✝

FOR REFLECTION: Exod. 23:13; Jer. 10:1-15; 44:24-27; Gal. 4:6-9; Rev. 2:14; 17:1-6; 21:8

125

The apostle Paul labels as a *heretic* anyone who chooses to adopt false doctrines for himself and then begins to teach them to others. Such a person is self-condemned. But we are not permitted to hold any doctrine created by our own will or to embrace anything someone else has produced out of his own fancy. In the teachings of the apostles we have our authority. But even the apostles did not of themselves introduce any doctrine, but they faithfully delivered to the nations the teaching they received from Christ. If, therefore, even "an angel from heaven should preach any other gospel" than that taught by the apostles, he must be accursed.

TERTULLIAN, *THE PRESCRIPTION AGAINST HERETICS*, CHAP. 6

ALMIGHTY GOD, you have revealed to your church your eternal Being of glorious majesty and perfect love as one God in Trinity of Persons: Give us grace to continue steadfast in the confession of this faith, and constant in our worship of you, Father, Son, and Holy Spirit; for you live and reign, one God, now and forever. Amen.

"OF THE HOLY TRINITY," COLLECTS: CONTEMPORARY, IN BCP

FOR REFLECTION: Deut. 13:1-4; Matt. 5:17-20; 7:15-20; 2 Cor. 11:14; **Gal. 1:8**; 5:20; Titus 3:10-11

126

Where heresy is found, there must first exist corruption of the Scriptures and their exposition. The Scriptures are the instruments of Christian doctrine. False teachers could not possibly have arrived at their heretical teaching in any other way than by manipulating the New Testament. Just as in their case, corruption of doctrine could not have succeeded without first abusing Scripture; even so, for us integrity of doctrine could not be kept without maintaining the integrity of Scripture, the safeguard of doctrine. Now, is there anything in the Scriptures contrary to how we Christians live? What of our own making have we introduced? What the Scriptures teach, that is what we are in our conduct and have been from the beginning. We were formed by the Scriptures before the heretics came along and added their erroneous constructions.

TERTULLIAN, *THE PRESCRIPTION AGAINST HERETICS*, CHAP. 38

THE CHURCH'S ONE FOUNDATION
Is Jesus Christ her Lord;
She is his new creation,
By water and the Word.
From heaven he came and sought her
To be his holy bride;
With his own blood he bought her,
And for her life he died. Amen.

SAMUEL JOHN STONE (1839–1900), HYMNARY

FOR REFLECTION: Jer. 2:8; 5:10-14; Rom. 16:17-18; 2 Cor. 2:16-17; 11:1-4; Eph. 4:14; 2 Tim. 3:13-17

127

(Tertullian summarizes his thoughts on the Lord's Prayer.)

In such few words, how many utterances of the prophets, the Gospels, the apostles, how many discourses, examples, parables of the Lord, are touched on! How many Christian duties are simultaneously discharged! Honoring God in the "our Father"; affirming the testimony of faith in God's "name"; offering obedience to God's "will"; commemorating hope in the "kingdom"; praying for life in the "bread"; acknowledging our debts in the petition for "forgiveness"; and admitting an anxious dread of temptation in the request for "protection." What wonder? God alone could teach us how we are to pray to him. The voicing of prayer, therefore, ordained by God and animated by the Holy Spirit, ascends to heaven, commending to the Father all that the Son has taught us.

TERTULLIAN, *ON PRAYER*, CHAP. 9

MY GOD, *I will extol thee*
And ever bless thy name;
Each day will I give thanks to thee
And all thy praise proclaim.
Great is the Lord and mighty,
And highly to be praised;
His greatness is unsearchable,
Above our knowledge raised. Amen.

THE PSALTER: WITH RESPONSIVE READINGS (1912), NO. 399, HYMNARY

FOR REFLECTION: Matt. 6:9-13; 26:39, 42, 44-75; **Luke 11:2-4**; John 17:1-26; Heb. 4:11-16

128

Where God is, there, too, is his child Patience. When God's Spirit descends, then Patience accompanies him. If we do not grant admission *to her* along with the Spirit, will he *continue* to tarry with us? Nay, I know not whether he would remain *any longer.* Without his companion and handmaid, he must of necessity be constricted in every place and at every time. Whatever blows his enemy might inflict, without Patience he would be unable to endure it. Patience is the instrumental means of endurance.

TERTULLIAN, *ON PATIENCE*, CHAP. 15

LEAD US, HEAVENLY FATHER, lead us
O'er the world's tempestuous sea;
Guard us, guide us, keep us, feed us,
For we have no help but thee;
Yet possessing every blessing,
If our God our Father be. Amen.

JAMES EDMESTON (1791–1867), HYMNARY

FOR REFLECTION: 1 Cor. 13:4-7; 2 Cor. 6:1-10; Gal. 5:22-26; Eph. 4:1-3; Col. 3:12-13; 2 Tim. 3:10-12

CYPRIAN OF CARTHAGE

In any grand mountain range there are majestic peaks that soar above others. The same holds true for the fathers who labored for the faith prior to the Council of Nicaea (AD 325). Cyprian of Carthage (Thascius Caecilius Cyprianus) (ca. AD 210-58) is a towering peak. While we should not overlook his shortcomings, in Cyprian's service to Christ and his church we recognize genius and sound judgment sanctified by the Holy Spirit and fully placed at God's disposal. As with Dietrich Bonhoeffer in the twentieth century, Cyprian had fully measured the cost of discipleship and did not shrink from its price. As the bishop of Carthage, he proved his mettle by the way he led amid storms that battered the church from the outside and from within. In the process, Cyprian articulated a doctrine of the church that, if it had been adhered to by the church in the West, might well have averted the rupture between the Eastern and Western wings of the church and might well have avoided conflicts that burst forth during the Protestant Reformation. Cyprian taught a doctrine of God's forgiveness that steered between cheap grace and quick access to the Lord's Table, on the one hand, and overbearing judgment and exclusion from true repentance, on the other.

Cyprian is eminent among that cast of leaders the church in North Africa produced. He was born in ca. AD 200 and was converted in AD 246 through the ministry of Caecilius. Because of Cyprian's love for Caecilius, at the time of his baptism Cyprian took the name of Caecilius, becoming known as Caecilius Cyprian. After surviving the great Decian persecution by fleeing Carthage (a decision that invited considerable criticism), Cyprian returned to his episcopal duties in AD 251. In AD 257 the eighth general persecution, initiated by Emperor Valerian, erupted. The fires of persecution raged in North Africa; thousands were martyred. Cyprian was arrested in August and was exiled to Curubis (current Korba, Tunisia). Recalled in AD 258, in September he was arrested and required to offer sacrifice to the gods. He refused and was sentenced to death. He was beheaded the following day.

Born to wealthy pagan parents, Cyprian was educated to become a teacher of rhetoric. On becoming a Christian, he gave the energies of his keen mind to studying the Christian faith, a study that paid rich dividends for the gospel—then and now. Shortly after Cyprian's conversion, he was ordained a presbyter (priest) and then soon bishop of Carthage (AD 248). Cyprian cared deeply for the poor and those who suffered because of their faith. He practiced what he preached. Shortly after his conversion, he sold his possessions and distributed the proceeds to those in need.

Cyprian was heavily influenced by Tertullian, as is revealed in his writings and theology. One of the many problems he and the other bishops confronted was how to deal with the lapsed who wanted to repent and return to the Lord's Table. Should penitent persons who had yielded to persecution by obtaining certificates that proved they had offered sacrifices to pagan deities be readmitted to Communion with the faithful? If so, under what conditions? Unlike some confessors, and Novatian (ca. AD 200-ca. 258), who opposed restoration of Communion and then proceeded to create his own "church," Cyprian believed the Lord's mercy should be extended to penitents. But restoration should occur only under carefully prescribed conditions agreed on by orthodox bishops.

Another major problem was whether baptism administered by heretics should be recognized as valid. Cyprian said, "Absolutely not!" Heretical bishops who have broken with the true church cannot legitimately baptize anyone; the sacraments are inseparable from the church. Persons baptized by heretics have in fact never been baptized; they would need to be baptized for the first time by an orthodox bishop. Cyprian declared, "He can no longer have God for his Father who has not the church for his mother" (*On the Unity of the Church*, para. 6). The church is the indispensable ark of salvation. Stephen, the bishop of Rome, disagreed and accepted baptism by heretical bishops. He even threatened to excommunicate Cyprian! Cyprian also taught that the unity of the church rests with orthodox bishops who constitute a college of equals and who regularly confer with each other through letters or in regional synods where doctrinal disagreements could be resolved. Parish clergy were to be included in the process. All decisions were to be guided by apostolic tradition, which belongs to the church alone, not to heretics. Cyprian would have firmly rejected the eventual Roman doctrine of the supreme pontiff or papacy to which other bishops must submit; he said the unity of the church rests with the several and equal bishops.

In some Cyprian pieces that follow we will hear him addressing "confessors." That was a title of honor designating the courageous champions of the faith who during times of persecution demonstrated loyalty to Christ by refusing to renounce him. Their stalwart confessions led to imperial punishment of various kinds: imprisonment, barbarous torture, exile and confiscation of property, and cruel labor in the Roman mines. The title distinguished the confessors from the martyrs, who were intentionally put to death. The term comes from the Latin word *confiteri* and was first employed by the Christians to identify their own. Of Cyprian's letters, some were written to confessors. He "refreshed their suffering breasts, healed their limbs wounded by clubs, and illuminated the darkness of their dungeon" (*Epistles of Cyprian,* epistle 77, para. 3).

Thankfully, we have most of Cyprian's rich letters and treatises, many of which were written while he was in exile. The following selections encourage us to love the Lord and his church just as intensely as did Cyprian.

129

(Cyprian tells of his conversion.)

While I was still lying in darkness and gloomy night, wavering hither and thither, tossed about on the foam of this boastful age, uncertain of my wandering steps, knowing nothing of my real life, and remote from truth and light, I used to regard it as a difficult matter, especially because of my character, that a person could be born again. While retaining all bodily structure, how could a person be changed in heart and soul? "How," said I, "is such a conversion possible, that there should be a sudden and rapid divestment of all that is either innate in us or has hardened in the corruption of our flesh, or has been acquired by long and persistent practice?" These were my frequent thoughts. For being held in bonds by my innumerable errors, I used to indulge my sins as if they were actually parts of me. But after that, by the help of the water of new birth, the stain of former years was washed away, and a light from above, serene and pure, was infused into my reconciled heart. By the agency of the Spirit, which was breathed into me from heaven, a second birth restored me to a new person.

CYPRIAN, *EPISTLE TO DONATUS*, PARAS. 3-4

My God, accept my heart this day,
And make it always thine,
That I from thee no more may stray,
No more from thee decline. Amen.

MATTHEW BRIDGES (1800-1894), HYMNARY

FOR REFLECTION: John 3:1-21; Acts 9:1-22; 26:1-29; 2 Cor. 6:9-11

130

(Cyprian describes life in the Spirit after his conversion.)

Then in a wondrous manner, doubtful things at once began to assure themselves to me, hidden things to be revealed and dark things to be enlightened. What before had seemed difficult began to yield to a means of accomplishment; what had been thought impossible, to be capable of being achieved, so I was enabled to acknowledge that what had previously (I being born of the flesh) been bound to the practice of sin (the earthly) had now begun to be of God, and was animated by the Spirit of holiness.

CYPRIAN, *EPISTLE TO DONATUS*, PARA. 4

DWELL IN ME, O blessed Spirit,
Gracious Teacher, Friend divine!
For the kingdom work that calls me,
O prepare this heart of mine.

Grant to me your sacred presence;
Then my faith will ne'er decline.
Comfort me and help me onward;
Fill with love this heart of mine. Amen.

FANNY CROSBY (1820–1915), HYMNARY

FOR REFLECTION: John 14:16; 1 Cor. 3:16; 6:19; 2 Cor. 3:2-3, 18; Gal. 5:22-25; Eph. 4:17-25; 2 Pet. 1:4; 1 John 3:24; 4:15

131

If you keep the way of innocence, the way of righteousness, if you walk with a firm and steady step, if, depending on God with your whole heart, you truly *be* what you have *begun to be,* then liberty and power to *do* will be given in proportion to the increase of your spiritual grace. For there is not, as characterizes earthly benefits, any limit in dispensing the heavenly gift. The Holy Spirit, flowing freely to us, is restrained by no limits. He is checked by no earthly barriers. The Spirit flows perpetually, is profuse in abundance. So let our hearts be athirst and ready to receive in the measure of an open faith, in the measure we wish to draw on God's overflowing grace.

CYPRIAN, *EPISTLE TO DONATUS*, PARA. 5

COME, GRACIOUS SPIRIT, heavenly Dove,
With light and comfort from above;
Be thou our Guardian, thou our Guide;
O'er every thought and step preside.

. . . . .

The light of truth to us display,
And make us know and choose thy way;
Plant holy fear in every heart,
That we from thee may ne'er depart.

Lead us to holiness, the road
That we must take to dwell with God;
Lead us to Christ, the living Way,
Nor let us from his pastures stray. Amen.

SIMON BROWNE (CA. 1680–1732), HYMNARY

FOR REFLECTION: Pss. 15:1-5; 24:3-5; 71:8; 112:4-8; Isa. 32:16-18; Rom. 8:4-6; 14:17-19; 15:1-7; 2 Cor. 7:1; Gal. 5:1, 16-26

132

Do you think that those who trust in wreaths of honor, in vast wealth, in the glitter of royal palaces, and in the safeguard of watchful arms are secure? They have greater fear than others. The power of those whom power makes terrible to others is first of all terrible to themselves. Power smiles at them in order to enrage them; it cajoles in order to deceive them; it entices to slay them; it lifts them up to cast them down. Their possessions amount to this only, that they can keep others from possessing them.

The one solid, firm, and constant security is this, for a person to reject these eddies of distraction. A Christian who is anchored in the harbor of salvation, who has received the gift of God, and who in his or her mind is very near to God is greater than the world. Such a person will crave nothing the world offers. How stable, how free from all shocks, is that safeguard; how heavenly the protection in its perennial blessings—to be loosed from the snares of this entangling world and fitted for the light of eternal immortality!

CYPRIAN, *EPISTLE TO DONATUS*, PARAS. 12-14

O LORD, save your people, and bless your inheritance, which you have purchased with the precious blood of your Christ. Feed them under your right hand, cover them under your wings, and grant that they may "fight the good fight and finish their course and keep the faith" immutably, blameless, and without reproach, through our Lord Jesus Christ, your beloved Son, with whom glory, honor, and worship be to you and to the Holy Spirit forever. Amen.

CONSTITUTIONS OF THE HOLY APOSTLES, BK. 8, SEC. 4.41

FOR REFLECTION: Rom. 8:1-28; **2 Tim. 4:7**; Heb. 10:19-25; 1 Pet. 1:3-9; 1 John 4:1-6

133

The more we understand the crafty mischief our foe directs against us, the more constrained we are to have more love for what we shall become as Christians and to condemn what we were before. To become what we will be as Christians through love, it is not necessary to pay a price of bribery or labor, as is required for being elevated in dignity and honor in this world. Instead, all of this is a gift from God, and it is accessible to all Christians.

As the sun shines spontaneously, as the day naturally gives light, as the fountain flows freely, as the shower yields moisture, so does the Holy Spirit give himself to us. When the soul, in its gaze into heaven, has recognized its Author, it rises higher than the sun, far transcends all earthly power, and begins to be that which it now knows itself to be.

CYPRIAN, *EPISTLE TO DONATUS*, PARA. 14

ALMIGHTY GOD, you have given your only Son to be for us a sacrifice for sin and also an example of godly life: Give us grace to receive thankfully the fruits of his redeeming work and to follow daily in the blessed steps of his most holy life; through Jesus Christ your Son our Lord, who lives and reigns with you and the Holy Spirit, one God, now and forever. Amen.

"PROPER 15," COLLECTS: CONTEMPORARY, IN BCP

FOR REFLECTION: Rom. 6:19-23; 8:14-28; Eph. 1:6-14; 3:14-21; Phil. 2:1-5; 3:7-16; Titus 3:3-7; 1 John 3:21-24; Rev. 21:5-7

134

You whom the celestial warfare has enlisted for service in the spiritual camp must observe a discipline uncorrupted and chastened in Christian virtues. Be constant in prayer and in reading the Scriptures. Speak with God, and let God speak with you. Let him instruct you in his precepts; let him direct you. Whom God has made rich, none can make poor. In fact, there can be no poverty for the one who has been fed heavenly food. Ceilings enriched with gold and houses adorned with mosaics of costly marble will seem small to you now that you are the one to be perfected, to be adorned. You are the dwelling in which God lives as in a temple. In you the Holy Spirit has begun to make his abode. Let us embellish this temple with the colors of innocence; let us enlighten it with the light of justice. This will never decay with the wear of age, nor will it be defiled by fading colors on the walls. All that is artificially beautified perishes. But the temple of the Holy Spirit remains beautiful perpetually. It can neither decay nor be destroyed; it can only be fashioned into greater perfection at the resurrection of the body.

CYPRIAN, *EPISTLE TO DONATUS*, PARA. 15

O LORD GOD ALMIGHTY, the Father of your Christ, your blessed Son, we thank you for the preservation of piety, for the remission of our offences, and for the name of your Christ by which we are joined to you. Gather all of us into your kingdom through this same Christ, our Lord, with whom glory, honor, and worship be to you, O Father, by the Holy Spirit, forever. Amen.

CLEMENTINE LITURGY (LATE FOURTH CENTURY), IN *CONSTITUTIONS OF THE HOLY APOSTLES*, BK. 8, SEC. 2.15

FOR REFLECTION: Matt. 5:14-16; Luke 6:46-49; 1 Cor. 6:19-20; Eph. 2:13-22; Heb. 12:12-15; 13:20-25; 1 John 4:7-19

135

(Cyprian's pastoral counsel to the confessors is timeless.)

In proportion as we grieve over those whom a hostile persecution has cast down, in the same proportion we rejoice over you whom the devil has not been able to overcome.

Yet I exhort you by our common faith, by the true and simple love of my heart toward you, that, having overcome the adversary in this first encounter, you must hold fast your victory with a brave and persevering virtue. We are still in the world; we are still placed in the battlefield; we fight daily for our lives. To what you have achieved with such a blessed commencement, there must now come an increase. What has commenced must be consummated. Even as faith and the new birth, which have been received, make us alive in Christ, they must be preserved. It is not the beginning but the perfecting that keeps a person for God. The Lord taught this in his instruction when he said, "Behold, you are made whole; sin no more, lest a worse thing come upon you." Think of him as saying, "Lo, you are made a confessor; sin no more, lest a worse thing come upon you."

CYPRIAN, *EPISTLE TO ROGATIANUS THE PRESBYTER, AND THE OTHER CONFESSORS*
(AD 250 AD), PARAS. 1-2

JESUS CALLS US FROM THE WORSHIP
Of the vain world's golden store;
From each idol that would keep us,
Saying, "Christian, love me more." Amen.

CECIL F. ALEXANDER (1818-95), HYMNARY

FOR REFLECTION: John 5:14; Gal. 1:6-11; 4:8-20; 5:1, 7-26; Heb. 2:1-4; 3:7–4:11; 6:18; 11:1–12:13; Jude vv. 17-25

136

Although there seem to be tares in the church, neither our faith nor our love should be hindered. Tares in the church should not cause us to forsake the church. Instead, let us labor to be wheat so that when the wheat is gathered into the Lord's barns, we will receive fruit for our labor. The apostle Paul tells us that "in a great house there are not only vessels of gold and silver but also of wood and of earth, and some to honor and some to dishonor." Let us strive, dearest brethren, and labor as much as we possibly can to be vessels of gold or silver. The servant cannot claim for himself what the Father has given to the Son alone; only the Son can take the winnowing fan and purge the threshing floor. By using human judgment the servant cannot correctly separate the tares from the wheat. Trying to do that shows proud obstinacy and sacrilegious presumption. We should always maintain moderation and let the Lord control the scales. Let us always be mindful of the love and mercy of God the Father.

CYPRIAN, *FROM CYPRIAN TO THE CONFESSORS, CONGRATULATING THEM ON THEIR RETURN FROM SCHISM*, PARA. 3

O LORD JESUS CHRIST, Son of the living God, Lamb and Shepherd, who takes away the sin of the world, who did freely forgive their debt to the two debtors and gave remission of her sins to the woman who was a sinner, who gave healing to the paralytic, with the remission of his sins, forgive, remit, pardon, O God, our offences. For, you are our God, a God able to pity, to save, and to forgive sins. All glory is due to you, with the eternal Father and the quickening Spirit, now and ever, and to all eternity. Amen.

THE DIVINE LITURGY OF JAMES THE HOLY APOSTLE (CA. AD 150–200)

FOR REFLECTION: Rom. 14:4; 1 Cor. 10:12; **2 Tim. 2:20**; 1 John 1:1-2

137

Let no Christian wonder why we are continually tried with increasing afflictions. The Lord told us these things would happen in the last times. He has prepared us for warfare by the teaching and exhortation of his words. The apostle Peter taught that persecutions occur for the sake of our being proved. He also said, by following the example of the righteous who have gone before, we should be joined to the love of God by death and sufferings. "Beloved, think it not strange concerning the fiery trial that is to try you, nor do you fall away, as if some new thing happened to you; but as often as you partake in Christ's sufferings, rejoice in all things, that when his glory shall be revealed, you may be glad also with exceeding joy. If you are reproached in the name of Christ, happy are you, for the majesty and power of the Lord rest on you."

CYPRIAN, *EPISTLE TO THE PEOPLE OF THIBARIS, EXHORTING TO MARTYRDOM*, PARA. 2

WE BESEECH YOU, O Lord our God, prepare us to receive your perfect lovingkindness; make straight our path: root us in your fear, and fit us for your heavenly kingdom, in Christ Jesus our Lord, with whom you are blessed, together with your all-holy, good, and quickening Spirit, now and forever. Amen.

THE DIVINE LITURGY OF JAMES THE HOLY APOSTLE (CA. AD 150–200)

FOR REFLECTION: Luke 6:22-23; 18:29-30; John 16:32-33; Acts 14:19-22; 2 Cor. 4:1–5:11; **1 Pet. 4:12-14**

138

We have not given ourselves to spiritual warfare in order to spend our time thinking about peace and then to retreat, refusing to engage the enemy. This is the warfare in which the Lord himself first engaged, he the Teacher of humility, endurance, and suffering. What he taught us to do, he himself first did. And what he exhorts us to suffer, he himself first suffered for us. Let it be clear, beloved brethren, that he who alone received all judgment from the Father, and who will come to judge, has already declared the criteria of his judgment and future recognition: he will confess before his Father those who confess him before people; he will deny those who deny him.

CYPRIAN, *EPISTLE TO THE PEOPLE OF THIBARIS, EXHORTING TO MARTYRDOM*, PARA. 3

WE RENDER THANKS TO YOU, the Savior and God of all, for all the good things you have given us and for our participation in your gospel. And we offer to you ourselves as a sweet savor of Christ to God the Father, praying: Keep us under the shadow of your wings and count us worthy till our last breath to partake of your holy gospel for the sanctification of our souls and bodies, for inheritance of the kingdom of heaven. For you, O God, are our sanctification, and we send up praise and thanksgiving to you, Father, Son, and Holy Spirit. Blessed are you, now and forever. Amen.

THE DIVINE LITURGY OF JAMES THE HOLY APOSTLE (CA. AD 150–200)

FOR REFLECTION: Jer. 9:1-3; Acts 5:31; 2 Cor. 1:1-5; 2:11; Eph. 1:12; 6:10-18; 1 Thess. 5:1-11; 1 Tim. 1:18-19; 6:12; 1 Pet. 4:6-11; 1 John 5:1-5

139

People train for secular contests, and they consider it great glory and honor when they are crowned in the presence of the populace and the emperor. Behold, we are engaged in a loftier and greater contest; it is glorious with the reward of a heavenly crown. God observes us in this struggle; he delights in our contest; he looks upon us in our warfare as we fight the good fight of faith. How great is the glory and happiness, having battled in God's presence, to be crowned by God with Christ as our judge! Let us be armed, beloved brethren, with our whole strength, and let us be prepared for the struggle with an uncorrupted mind, with a sound faith, with a devoted courage. Let the camp of God go forth to the battlefield that is appointed to us.

CYPRIAN, *EPISTLE TO THE PEOPLE OF THIBARIS, EXHORTING TO MARTYRDOM*, PARA. 8

O GOD, who through your great and unspeakable love did condescend to the weakness of us your servants and has in the gospel given us eternal life, preserve us in the sanctification of your Holy Spirit, that being made holy, we may find part and inheritance with all your saints that have been well-pleasing to you since the world began, in the light of your countenance, through the mercy of your only begotten Son, our Lord and God and Savior Jesus Christ, with whom you are blessed, together with your all-holy, good, and quickening Spirit; for blessed and glorified is your all-precious and glorious name, Father, Son, and Holy Spirit, now and to all eternity. Amen.

THE DIVINE LITURGY OF JAMES THE HOLY APOSTLE (CA. AD 150–200)

FOR REFLECTION: Jer. 9:1-3; Acts 5:31; 2 Cor. 1:5; 2:11; Eph. 1:12; 6:10-18; 1 Thess. 5:1-11; 1 Tim. 1:18-19; 6:12; 1 Pet. 4:6-11; 1 John 5:1-5

140

How grave is the case of a Christian if that person, a servant of Christ, is unwilling to suffer when his or her Master suffered for us! The Son of God suffered that he might make us children of God, and will we not suffer that we may continue to be the children of God? If we suffer the world's hatred, Christ first endured the world's hatred. If we suffer the world's reproaches, if exile, if tortures, the Maker and Lord of the world experienced harder things than these. He warns us, saying, "If the world hates you, remember that it hated me before it hated you." "The servant is not greater than his lord. If they have persecuted me, they will also persecute you." Whatever our Lord and God taught us to do, he first did himself. His disciples will not be excused if they learn but do not follow him.

CYPRIAN, *EPISTLE TO THE PEOPLE OF THIBARIS, EXHORTING TO MARTYRDOM*, PARA. 6

LORD JESU, *think on me,*
    And purge away my sin;
From earthborn passions set me free,
    And make me pure within.

Lord Jesu, *think on me,*
    With care and woe oppressed;
Let me thy loving servant be,
    And taste thy promised rest. Amen.

SYNESIUS OF CYRENE, BISHOP OF PTOLEMAIS (CA. AD 370–CA. 414), TRANS.
ALLEN W. CHATFIELD (1876)

FOR REFLECTION: John 15:18-25; Rom. 8:16-28; 2 Cor. 1:3-10; 4:5-14; Phil. 1:27–2:4; 3:8-14; 2 Tim. 2:8-13; 1 Pet. 4:12-19

141

(In the autumn of AD 250, Cyprian wrote to confessors laboring in Roman mines. They were beginning their second year of imprisonment.)

Behold, the heavenly dignity in you is sealed by the brightness of a year's honor. The rising sun and the waning moon have enlightened the outside world; but for you, the God who created the sun and moon has been a brighter light in your dungeon. And the brightness of Christ glowing in your hearts and minds has irradiated with eternal and brilliant light the gloom of your punishment. The winter has passed through the vicissitudes of the months. But you, imprisoned, instead of undergoing the inclement weather of winter, were experiencing the winter of persecution. Spring followed winter, rejoicing with roses and crowned with flowers. But to you in prison were given the roses and flowers that spring from the delights of paradise, and celestial garlands wreathed your brows.

CYPRIAN, *EPISTLE TO MOYSES AND MAXIMUS, AND THE REST OF THE CONFESSORS,*
PARA. 2

O HEAVENLY FATHER, who has filled the world with beauty: Open our eyes to behold your gracious hand in all your works; that, rejoicing in your whole creation, we may learn to serve you with gladness; for the sake of him through whom all things were made, your Son Jesus Christ our Lord. Amen.

"FOR JOY IN GOD'S CREATION," PRAYERS AND THANKSGIVINGS, IN BCP

FOR REFLECTION: Luke 6:20-23; 21:7-19; John 15:18-27; 2 Cor. 4:8-12; 1 John 3:1-3

142

You are grains of wheat, winnowed and precious corn, now purged and garnered. Regard your prison as a granary. There is no lack of the spiritual grace needed to discharge the duties of the harvest season. Outside, the grape that shall hereafter flow into the cups is now being trodden in the presses. You, rich bunches from the Lord's vineyard, and branches with fruit already ripened, trodden by tribulation, now fill the wine-press with your blood instead of wine. Brave to bear suffering, you willingly drink the cup of martyrdom. Truly, you gospel witnesses, you Christ's martyrs, are grounded in his roots. You are established on the Rock, who is your strong foundation. You have joined discipline to virtue; you have led others to fear God; of your martyrdoms you have made examples.

CYPRIAN, *EPISTLE TO MOYSES AND MAXIMUS, AND THE REST OF THE CONFESSORS,* PARA. 2, 4

O GOD, you made us in your own image and redeemed us through Jesus your Son: Look with compassion on the whole human family; take away the arrogance and hatred that infect our hearts; break down the walls that separate us; unite us in bonds of love; and work through our struggle and confusion to accomplish your purposes on earth; that, in your good time, all nations and races may serve you in harmony around your heavenly throne; through Jesus Christ our Lord. Amen.

"FOR THE HUMAN FAMILY," PRAYERS AND THANKSGIVINGS, IN BCP

FOR REFLECTION: Pss. 23:1-6; 34:1-8; 37:1-11; 40:1-5; 43:1-5; Isa. 53:1-9; Heb. 12:1-3; 13:12-16; Rev. 21:1-7

143

The church is one. It is spread abroad far and wide into a multitude by an increase of fruitfulness. As there are many rays of the sun, but one light; many branches of a tree, but one strength based in its tenacious root; and many streams flowing, but one spring, so unity is preserved in the source. Cut off the stream from its fountain, and that which is cut off dries up. Thus also the church, shone over by the light of the Lord, sheds her rays over the whole world; yet one light is everywhere diffused. Her fruitful abundance spreads her branches over the whole world. She broadly expands her rivers, liberally flowing, yet her head is one, her source one; and she is one mother, plentiful in the results of fruitfulness: from her womb we are born, by her milk we are nourished, by her spirit we are animated.

CYPRIAN, *ON THE UNITY OF THE CHURCH*, PARA. 5

ETERNAL GOD, in whose perfect kingdom no sword is drawn but the sword of righteousness, no strength known but the strength of love: So mightily spread abroad your Spirit, that all peoples may be gathered under the banner of the Prince of Peace, as children of one Father; to whom be dominion and glory, now and forever. Amen.

"FOR PEACE," PRAYERS AND THANKSGIVINGS, IN BCP

FOR REFLECTION: Isa. 60:21; Acts 20:28; 1 Cor. 3:5-12; Eph. 1:22-23; Heb. 12:22-23; 1 Pet. 5:3; Rev. 21:11

144

The church, the spouse of Christ, keeps us for God. Whoever is separated from the church and is joined to an adulteress is separated from the promises of the church; nor can he who forsakes the church of Christ attain to the rewards of Christ. He is a stranger; he is profane; he is an enemy. He can no longer have God for his Father who has not the church for his mother. If anyone could escape who was outside the ark of Noah, then he also can escape who shall be outside the church. The one who breaks the peace and the concord of Christ does so in opposition to Christ; he who gathers elsewhere than in the church scatters the church of Christ. It is written of the Father and of the Son and of the Holy Spirit, "And these three are one." Does one believe that the unity of the church can be divided and splintered by opposing wills? He who does not hold this unity does not hold God's law, does not hold the faith of the Father and the Son, and does not hold to life and salvation.

CYPRIAN, *On the Unity of the Church*, PARA. 6

O GOD, who made this most holy night to shine with the glory of the Lord's resurrection: Stir up in your church that Spirit of adoption that is given to us in baptism, that we, being renewed both in body and mind, may worship you in sincerity and truth; through Jesus Christ our Lord, who lives and reigns with you, in the unity of the Holy Spirit, one God, now and forever. Amen.

"EASTER DAY," COLLECTS: CONTEMPORARY, IN BCP

FOR REFLECTION: John 10:1-18; Rom. 12:3-10; 2 Cor. 6:6; Eph. 1:17-23; 2:9; 4:1-16; 5:13-24; 1 Tim. 3:14-16; Heb. 12:22-24; **1 John 5:7**

145

We ought to lay aside everything except the whole armor of God, lest when the day of going forth to meet Christ comes, it should find us burdened and entangled. Let our light shine in good works and glow so brightly as to lead us from the night of this world to the daylight of eternal brightness. Let us always with concern for the well-being of others, and with caution, wait for the sudden coming of the Lord, that when he shall knock, our faith may be on the watch and receive from the Lord the reward of our vigilance. If these commands be observed, if these warnings and precepts be kept, we cannot be overtaken in slumber by the deceit of the devil; but we shall reign with Christ in his kingdom as servants that keep watch.

CYPRIAN, *ON THE UNITY OF THE CHURCH*, PARA. 27

ALMIGHTY AND EVERLASTING GOD, you are always more ready to hear than we to pray, and to give more than we either desire or deserve: Pour on us the abundance of your mercy, forgiving us those things of which our conscience is afraid, and giving us those good things for which we are not worthy to ask, except through the merits and mediation of Jesus Christ our Savior, who lives and reigns with you and the Holy Spirit, one God, forever and ever. Amen.

"PROPER 22," COLLECTS: CONTEMPORARY, IN BCP

FOR REFLECTION: Matt. 25:1-46; 26:36-46; Mark 13:28-37; Eph. 6:13-18; Phil. 4:4-9; 1 Thess. 5:4-11

146

We pray, "Hallowed be your name." This does not mean that we want to make God holy by our prayers. Instead, we pray that his name will be hallowed in us. By whom is God to be sanctified? He is the One who sanctifies. Well, because God commands us, "Be holy, even as I am holy." We petition that we who were sanctified in baptism may continue to be what we began to be. For this we pray daily, for we have need of daily sanctification, that we who daily need forgiveness may be cleansed by continual sanctification. We are made holy in the name of our Lord Jesus Christ and by the Spirit of our God. We pray that this sanctification may abide in us. We make this supplication in constant prayer, that the sanctification and quickening that we receive by God's grace will be preserved by his protection.

CYPRIAN, *ON THE LORD'S PRAYER*, PARA. 12

OH! FOR A CLOSER WALK WITH GOD,
 A calm and heavenly frame;
A light to shine upon the road
 That leads me to the Lamb!

 . . . .

The dearest idol I have known,
 Whate'er that idol be,
Help me to bear it from thy throne,
 And worship only thee. Amen.

WILLIAM COWPER (1731–1800), HYMNARY

FOR REFLECTION: Lev. 20:7; **Matt. 6:9-13**; **Luke 11:2-4**; Gal. 3:19-21; 5:16-21; Eph. 4:14-16; Col. 3:1-17; 1 Thess. 4:1-8; 2 Thess. 2:13-17

147

There follows in the prayer, "Your kingdom come." Our prayer is that the kingdom of God will be established in us, even as we ask that God's name be sanctified in us. But when does God begin to reign? Hasn't he always reigned, and will he not always reign? Our prayer is that the kingdom promised by God and acquired through the blood and passion of Christ may come in its fullness. Christ himself, dearest brethren, is the kingdom of God whom we day by day desire to come, whose advent we crave to be quickly manifested. He is the Resurrection, and in him we rise again.

CYPRIAN, *On the Lord's Prayer*, PARA. 13

Almighty and everlasting God, in Christ you have revealed your glory among the nations: Preserve the works of your mercy, that your church throughout the world may persevere with steadfast faith in the confession of your name; through Jesus Christ our Lord, who lives and reigns with you and the Holy Spirit, one God, forever and ever. Amen.

"Proper 24," Collects: Contemporary, in BCP

FOR REFLECTION: Matt. 4:23; **6:9-15**; 9:35; Mark 1:1-15; **Luke** 4:1-30; **11:2-4**; 1 Cor. 15:12-58

148

Jesus petitioned the Father, saying, "Neither pray I for these alone, but for them also that shall believe on me through their word." The Lord's loving-kindness, no less than his mercy, is great in respect to our salvation; not content to redeem us with his blood, he also prayed for us. For what did he pray? Just as the Father and Son are one, even so Christians should abide in absolute unity. From this it may be understood how greatly one sins who ruptures unity and peace. The Lord desired that his people should be saved and live in peace; he knew that discord cannot enter the kingdom of God.

CYPRIAN, *On the Lord's Prayer*, PARA. 30

GOD OF MERCY, *God of grace,*
Show the brightness of your face;
Shine upon us, Savior, shine;
Fill your church with light divine;
And your saving health extend
Unto earth's remotest end.

. . . .

Let the people praise you, Lord;
Earth shall then its fruits afford,
God to us all blessings give,
We to God devoted live;
All below and all above
One in joy and light and love. Amen.

HENRY FRANCIS LYTE (1793–1847), HYMNARY

FOR REFLECTION: John 17:1-26; Rom. 15:5-7; 1 Cor. 12:3-31

149

Many and great, beloved brethren, are the divine benefits for which the abundant mercy of God the Father and Christ has labored and is always laboring. The Father sent the Son to preserve us and give us life so that he might restore us. The Son was willing to be sent and to become the Son of Man, that he might make us children of God; he humbled himself, that he might raise up the people who before were prostrate; he was wounded, that he might heal our wounds; he served, that he might bring to liberty those who once were in bondage; he underwent death, that he might grant immortality to mortals.

CYPRIAN, *ON WORKS AND ALMS*, PARA. 1

CHRIST, of all my hopes the Ground,
Christ, the Spring of all my joy,
Still in you may I be found,
Still for you my powers employ.

Let your love my heart inflame;
Keep your fear before my sight;
Be your praise my highest aim;
Be your smile my chief delight! Amen.

A COLLECTION OF HYMNS FOR THE USE OF THE PEOPLE CALLED METHODISTS (1889), HYMN 672

FOR REFLECTION: Pss. 18:46-50; 108:1-6; John 1:6-13; 14:12-21; Heb. 4:14-16; 1 Pet. 1:3-16; 1 John 1:7-9

150

What, dearest brethren, will be that glory of those who labor charitably? How great and high our joy when the Lord begins to number his people and begins to give heavenly things for earthly, eternal things for temporal, great things for small? How great and high our joy when Christ presents us to the Father, to whom he has restored us through sanctification. The Father will bestow on us immortality and eternity, for which he has renewed us by the quickening of his blood. He will bring us anew to paradise and will open the kingdom of heaven in fulfillment of his promises! Let these things abide firmly in our thoughts; let them be understood with full faith; and let them be loved with our whole heart. An illustrious and divine thing, dearest brethren, is the saving labor of charity—the true and greatest gift of God, needful for the weak, and glorious for the strong.

CYPRIAN, *ON WORKS AND ALMS*, PARA. 26

LET US PRAY for those who bear fruit in the holy church and give alms to the needy. And let us pray for those who offer sacrifices and oblations to the Lord our God, that God, the Fountain of all goodness, may recompense them with his heavenly gifts and "give them in this world a hundredfold and in the world to come life everlasting" and that he may bestow upon them for their temporal things, those that are eternal. Let us pray for our brethren newly enlightened, that the Lord may strengthen and confirm them. Let us pray for our brethren exercised with sickness, that the Lord may deliver them and restore them sound into his holy church. Amen.

CLEMENTINE LITURGY (LATE FOURTH CENTURY), IN *CONSTITUTIONS OF THE HOLY APOSTLES*, BK. 8, SEC. 2.10

FOR REFLECTION: Pss. 1–2; 112:5-10; Isa. 58:6-7; **Matt.** 5:42; 6:1-4; **19:29**; Luke 16:19-31; Rom. 12:8-13; 1 Tim. 6:17-19; James 2:14-16; 5:1-9

151

Patience is a mark of God's character. Christians who are gentle, patient, and meek imitate God the Father. Jesus Christ, our God and Lord, taught this in his words and deeds. Among the many virtues by which he demonstrated divine majesty, in patience he revealed the Father. He descended from heavenly sublimity to earthly things and did not scorn to assume human flesh. Although he was sinless, he bore the sins of others. Laying aside his immortality, he permitted himself to become mortal so that the guiltless could be put to death to save the guilty. He submitted to being baptized by his servant. For forty days he suffered famine so that all who hunger for the word of God and for grace might feast upon Christ the heavenly Bread. He ruled over his disciples not as servants under a master's power, but kindly and gently he loved them with a brotherly love. He deigned even to wash their feet so that by his example he might teach what a fellow servant ought to be among his peers and equals.

CYPRIAN, ON THE ADVANTAGE OF PATIENCE, PARAS. 5-6

HAIL, THOU ONCE DESPISED JESUS!
Hail, thou Galilean King!
Thou didst suffer to release us;
Thou didst free salvation bring.
Hail, thou agonizing Savior,
Bearer of our sin and shame!
By thy merits we find favor;
Life is given through thy name. Amen.

A COLLECTION OF HYMNS FOR THE USE OF THE PEOPLE CALLED METHODISTS (1889), HYMN 722

FOR REFLECTION: Isa. 29:14; Matt. 26:55–27:50; Luke 4:1-13; Phil. 2:5-10; Col. 2:8, 10; Heb. 2:9-12

152

He in whose name the devil and his angels are now being scourged once himself suffered scourging. He who was crowned with thorns now crowns martyrs with eternal flowers. He who was stripped of his earthly garments now clothes others in the vesture of immortality. He who was offered gall now offers heavenly food. He who was given vinegar to drink now appoints the cup of salvation. He who shall judge was judged; the Word of God was led silently to the slaughter. And after all these things, he still forgives his murderers if they will be converted and come to him. With a saving patience, he who is gracious to preserve closes his church to no one.

CYPRIAN, *On the Advantage of Patience*, PARAS. 7-8

O God, the Father of all, whose Son commanded us to love our enemies: Lead them and us from prejudice to truth; deliver them and us from hatred, cruelty, and revenge; and in your good time enable us all to stand reconciled before you; through Jesus Christ our Lord. Amen.

"FOR OUR ENEMIES," PRAYERS AND THANKSGIVINGS, IN BCP

FOR REFLECTION: Isa. 53:4-9; Matt. 27:26-56; John 19:1-40; Acts 2:22-24; Heb. 2:6-18

153

What shall I say of anger, of discord, of strife, which should not be found in a Christian? Let there be patience in the breast, and these things will not find a place there. If they try to enter, they will be quickly excluded, and they will depart so that a peaceful abode will characterize the heart where the God of peace delights to dwell. If a Christian has abandoned rage and carnal contention as one escapes hurricanes, and is tranquil and meek in the harbor of Christ, that Christian ought to admit neither anger nor discord to the breast.

CYPRIAN, *On the Advantage of Patience*, PARA. 16

BE NOT FAR FROM ME, *O my Strength,*
Whom all my times obey;
Take from me anything thou wilt;
But go not thou away—
And let the storm that does thy work
Deal with me as it may.

. . . .

Happy are they that learn, in thee,
Though patient suffering teach,
The secret of enduring strength,
And praise too deep for speech—
Peace that no pressure from without,
No strife within, can reach. Amen.

ANNA LETITIA WARING (1823–1910), HYMNARY

FOR REFLECTION: Rom. 14:1–15:7; 1 Cor. 12:1-31; 2 Cor. 6:4; 10:1-5; Heb. 10:36; 12:1

154

Patience commends and keeps us to God. It assuages anger, bridles the tongue, governs the mind, protects peace, governs discipline, breaks the power of lust, represses the violence of pride, extinguishes the fire of enmity, checks the power of the rich, soothes the want of the poor, protects the integrity of virgins and purity in widows, and insures a single affection in the married. Patience makes people humble in prosperity, brave in adversity, and gentle toward wrongs. It teaches us to pardon those who wrong us and to petition long and earnestly when we do wrong. Patience resists temptations, suffers persecutions, and perfects passions and martyrdoms. It is patience that fortifies our faith and elevates our hope. It directs what we do so that we may hold fast to the way of Christ. Patience will preserve us as God's children, providing that we imitate our Father's patience.

CYPRIAN, *On the Advantage of Patience*, PARA. 20

O MASTER, let me walk with thee
In lowly paths of service free;
Tell me thy secret: help me bear
The strain of toil, the fret of care.

. . . .

Teach me thy patience—still with thee
In closer, dearer company,
In work that keeps faith sweet and strong,
In trust that triumphs over wrong. Amen.

WASHINGTON GLADDEN (1836–1918), HYMNARY

✦✦✦

FOR REFLECTION: Col. 1:11; 1 Thess. 1:3; 5:21; 2 Thess. 1:4; 1 Tim. 6:11; Heb. 10:23; Rev. 2:25; 3:3

155

How great is the Lord Jesus, and how great is his patience: he who is worshipped in heaven is not yet worshipped on earth! Let us, beloved brethren, consider his patience in our persecutions and sufferings; let us give an obedience full of expectation for his coming; and let us not hasten, servants as we are, to seek our defense through unrighteous and immodest impulsiveness. Instead, let us press on and labor. Watching with our whole heart, and steadfast in endurance, let us keep the Lord's precepts so that when the day of judgment comes we will not be punished with the impious and sinners but may be numbered among the righteous, with those who fear God.

CYPRIAN, *ON THE ADVANTAGE OF PATIENCE*, PARA. 24

O SACRED HEAD, now wounded,
With grief and shame bowed down,
Now scornfully surrounded
With thorns, thine only crown.
O sacred Head, what glory,
What bliss till now was thine!
Yet, though despised and gory,
I joy to call thee mine. Amen.

ATTRIBUTED TO BERNARD OF CLAIRVAUX (1090–1153), TRANS. PAUL GERHARDT (1656) AND JAMES W. ALEXANDER (1830), HYMNARY

FOR REFLECTION: Isa. 53:1-12; 1 Thess. 5:1-28; 1 Tim. 6:13-21; 2 Tim. 4:1-8; Heb. 13:13-21

THE EASTERN CHURCH
AFTER ORIGEN AND
BEFORE NICAEA

After Origen, the church in the eastern part of the Roman Empire was characterized in many ways by his theology. Even those who opposed Origen, like Methodius of Olympus, were nevertheless influenced by him. Justo González notes that even after some of Origen's ideas were condemned, his works continued to be read and some aspects of his theology were widespread. In short, as González observes, "the main theological schools were really various factions of the Master."*

Among notable figures in Alexandria who continued Origen's legacy were Bishop Heraclas (serving from AD 232 to 248); Dionysius the Great, whom we included in the School of Alexandria; theologian Theognostus (ca. AD 210-70); and Pierius of Alexandria (d. ca. AD 309 in Rome). Origenists in Caesarea included Pamphilus, bishop of Caesarea (martyred in AD 309), who enlarged the library Origen had founded there. Another was the church historian Eusebius of Caesarea (ca. AD 263–339), who became bishop of Caesarea (ca. AD 313). He called himself Eusebius Pamphili, son of Pamphilus, because of his

*Justo González, *A History of Christian Thought* (Nashville: Abingdon Press, 1970), 1:253.

devotion to Bishop Pamphilus, who had ordained him a presbyter. Eusebius was able to write his *Ecclesiastical History* largely because of the resources Origen's expanded library offered. Still another disciple of Origen was Gregory of Neocaesarea, whom we will meet momentarily. As mentioned earlier, an Eastern father who was not a disciple of Origen was Methodius, whose works we will also explore.

During the third century prior to the Council of Nicaea, two heresies associated with the doctrine of the Trinity appeared in the East. The *first* heresy emerged from the thinking of Paul of Samosata, who became bishop of Antioch around AD 260. His strong interest in preserving the monotheistic unity of God—perhaps motivated by his political liabilities—came at the expense of maintaining a correct distinction between the Father, the Son, and the Holy Spirit. His extreme distinction between the Father and the Son meant that only the Father is God. The Logos (Word) is a virtue or characteristic of the Father, not a second person, as orthodox Trinitarian doctrine would resolutely affirm. Because there was no eternal second person of the Trinity there could be no real incarnation in Jesus of Nazareth. What Paul of Samosata taught about the Holy Spirit is not clear. But it is obvious he did not consider the Holy Spirit a third person of the Trinity. Although it was difficult to pin Paul down, his teachings were considered and condemned, and he was finally deposed after three synods held at Antioch (AD 265-69).

Arianism was the *second* heresy. It arose in the teaching of Arius (d. AD 336), a native of Libya and a presbyter (AD 313) in the church of Alexandria. As a priest, Arius expounded the Scriptures in a way that denied the deity of Christ. He taught that before time the Son was God's first creation. "The Son has a beginning, but God is without beginning" (Arius's letter to Eusebius of Nicomedia, ca. AD 319). After creating the Son, God created everything else through the Son. He is above all other creatures and is their Savior. Like Paul of Samosata, Arius believed that he was protecting monotheistic unity. Though condemned in the Council of Nicaea, Arianism would continue to plague the church (especially in the East) for decades afterward. In the second volume of this series we will see how the fathers confronted Arianism and settled questions Arius had raised.

GREGORY OF NEOCAESAREA

A most intriguing Eastern father was Gregory of Neocaesarea (ca. AD 213-ca. 270), also known as Gregory Thaumaturgus (Wonder-Worker). He received this name because it was believed he had been given the power to perform miracles in service to the gospel. Gregory was bishop of Neocaesarea from approximately AD 213 until his death in AD 275. He was born of wealthy pagan parents in Neocaesarea, the chief city of the province of Pontus. In a work that praises Origen (*Oration and Panegyric Addressed to Origen*), Gregory tells us that after his father's death, when he was fourteen, the "sacred Word" began to visit him and draw him to salvation. Looking back, Gregory could see how God's "holy and marvelous providence" had led him.

After completing his study of rhetoric and law (ca. AD 233), and after five years of study under Origen in Caesarea, where he was converted and baptized, Gregory returned to his native city and became part of a small group of Christians. Origen wrote a letter urging Gregory to dedicate himself to Christ as a presbyter (priest). While Gregory was away from the city for prayer and reflection, Phaedimus, bishop of Amasea, made him bishop of Neocaesarea (ca. AD 240). Yielding reluctantly, Gregory began a remarkable tenure as a wise and loving episcopal servant, and he became an effective missionary. He also led his congregation through the Decian persecution (AD 250) and during an invasion by the Goths from the north (ca. AD 260).

In addition to the *Oration and Panegyric Addressed to Origen*, Gregory's recognized extant works are *A Declaration of Faith* (in which he affirms that the "Trinity *abideth* ever"), *A Metaphrase* (word-for-word translation) *of Ecclesiastes*, and the *Canonical Epistle* (instructions in Christian discipline and repentance during perilous times).

156

(During the reign of Gallienus [AD 259-67] the Goths ravaged many cities in the province of Asia. To stem the resulting disorder in the church, Gregory sent his Canonical Epistle *to deal with Christians who were exploiting the terrible events to seize the property of other Christians who had fled or been captured. His epistle is an enduring warning against covetousness.)*

Covetousness is a great evil. Many scriptures condemn robbery and the grasping mind. They also condemn the disposition to meddle with what belongs to others to satisfy one's sordid love for gain. Some Christians have been so brazen as to use the destruction caused by the Goths as an opportunity for their own aggrandizement. They have made themselves marauding barbarians to others. Only people who hate God and who are given to unsurpassable iniquity do such things. It seems good to excommunicate such persons, "lest the impious work the destruction of the righteous" and the wrath of God fall on us all—especially on those placed in church office. If the Scriptures condemn aggrandizing oneself at the expense of another in the time of peace, how much more must this be true when one is met by adversity?

GREGORY OF NEOCAESAREA, *CANONICAL EPISTLE*, CANONS 2, 4, 5, 10

TEACH ME, O LORD, *your holy way,*
And give me an obedient mind;
That in your service I may find
My soul's delight from day to day. Amen.

WILLIAM TIDD MATSON (1833-99), HYMNARY

✦✦✦

FOR REFLECTION: Gen. 18:23, 25; Exod. 23:4; Deut. 22:1-3; Jer. 6:13-15; Rom. 1:28-32; 1 Cor. 13:4-7; Eph. 5:3-5; Phil. 2:5-15; James 4:1-10; 2 Pet. 2:14-16; 1 John 2:15-17

METHODIUS OF OLYMPUS

Regrettably, we know little about Methodius (d. ca. AD 311). Eusebius of Caesarea omitted all discussion of him in his *Ecclesiastical History*. This was probably because Eusebius revered Origen, while Methodius strongly opposed some of Origen's teachings. Jerome (ca. AD 340–420), who provides much of what we know about Methodius, states he was bishop of Olympus, a city in Syria. He was martyred in about AD 311 during the persecution instigated by Emperor Diocletian (r. AD 284–305), the final and most intense of all the general persecutions. Persecution was most severe in the eastern provinces. Two years after Methodius's martyrdom, Emperors Constantine (West) and Licinius Augustus (East) would issue the Edict of Milan, which granted religious freedom to Christians throughout the empire and restored church property that had been confiscated.

Methodius was doctrinally solid and an elegant and painstaking writer. Plato was his model. He often used dialogue to argue his positions. Although he was a staunch opponent of the theology of Origen, he was nevertheless influenced by him. Methodius opposed Origen's belief in the preexistence of the soul and the eternity of the world, Origen's use of allegory for biblical interpretation, and his teaching on eschatology (last things). Origen's way of describing the Son's subordination to the Father, which Methodius opposed, would be corrected at the Council of Nicaea (AD 325).

157

According to Greek legend, when Ulysses wanted to hear the song of the Sirens, he sailed to Sicily in bonds because of the Sirens' beguiling music. He filled the sailors' ears with wax so they could not hear. Death was the consequence of those who were lured to the shoals by the Sirens' music. Now, I am not within the hearing of any such song as that sung by the Sirens. Nor do I have any desire to listen to their music. But I do pray to enjoy the pleasure of the divine voice that, though it be often heard, I long to hear again. Not that I am overcome by the charm of a voluptuous voice, but I am being taught divine mysteries and expect the result to be not death but eternal salvation. The singers of this music are not the deadly Sirens of the Greeks but a divine choir of prophets with whom there is no need to stop the ears of one's companions. Nor is there any need to bind oneself with chains in fear of the penalty of hearing. In the first instance the one who hears the music dies. But the more one hears the chorus of prophets, the more one enjoys a better life, for that person is being led onward by the Holy Spirit.

METHODIUS, *CONCERNING FREE WILL*, A DIALOGUE BETWEEN ORTHODOXUS AND VALENTINIAN

SANCTIFY ALSO, O LORD, our souls, bodies, and spirits and touch our understandings, search our consciences, and cast out from us every motion of the flesh and spirit that is not in accordance with your holy will. And count us worthy, O loving Lord, with boldness, without condemnation, in a pure heart, with a contrite spirit, with unashamed face, and with sanctified lips to dare to call upon you, the Holy God, Father in heaven. Amen.

THE DIVINE LITURGY OF JAMES THE HOLY APOSTLE (CA. AD 150–200)

FOR REFLECTION: Matt. 13:44-46; Luke 19:1-10; 24:13-34; Gal. 5:22-26; Titus 2:11-14

158

Let everyone come, then, and hear without fear the divine song. There are not with us the Sirens from the shore of Sicily, nor the bonds of Ulysses, nor melted wax poured into our ears, but a casting off of all chains, and freedom to listen for all who desire to hear the divine song. It is good to hear such a song as this. To listen to such singers seems to me to be a thing to be sought in prayer. If one wishes to hear the choir of the apostles, he will find the same harmony of song in them as is found in the prophets. For the prophets sang beforehand the divine plan, but the apostles sing an interpretation of what the prophets announced. Oh, concordant harmony, composed by the Divine Spirit! Oh, the beauty of those who sing of the mysteries of God! Oh, that I, too, may join in these songs in my prayers. Let us then also sing this song and raise a hymn to the Holy Father, glorifying Jesus in the Spirit.

METHODIUS, *CONCERNING FREE WILL,*
A DIALOGUE BETWEEN ORTHODOXUS AND VALENTINIAN

MORTALS, JOIN THE MIGHTY CHORUS,
Which the morning stars began;
God's own love is reigning o'er us,
Joining people hand in hand.
Ever singing, march we onward,
Victors in the midst of strife;
Joyful music leads us sunward
In the triumph song of life. Amen.

HENRY VAN DYKE (1852–1933), HYMNARY

FOR REFLECTION: Isa. 55:1-3; 61:1-3; 63:7-9; John 1:18; Rom. 5:1-21; Eph. 5:1-2; Col. 1:1-14

159

Do not shun a spiritual hymn, nor be ill-disposed to listen to it. Death, as it was for the Greek sailors, belongs not to the choir of the apostles. Their song is the story of salvation. Already I seem to taste the better enjoyments as I discourse on such subjects as these, especially when there lies before me the flowering meadow, that is, the assembly of those who unite in singing and hearing the divine mysteries. O noble audience and venerable company and spiritual food! Oh, that I may ever have a right to share in such pleasures; be this my prayer!

METHODIUS, CONCERNING FREE WILL,
A DIALOGUE BETWEEN ORTHODOXUS AND VALENTINIAN

PRAISE THE LORD: *ye heavens, adore him;*
Praise him, angels, in the height;
Sun and moon, rejoice before him;
Praise him, all ye stars of light.
Praise the Lord, for he hath spoken;
Worlds his mighty voice obeyed.
Laws that never shall be broken
For their guidance he hath made. Amen.

ANONYMOUS (CA. 1801), HYMNARY

FOR REFLECTION: Luke 1:47; John 15:9, 11-17; 16:20-22; Acts 11:18; 16:25; Rom. 5:2; Phil. 3:1; 1 Thess. 5:16; 1 Pet. 1:8-9

160

(Of the fathers who wrote before the Council of Nicaea, Methodius provides the most extensive discussion of the origin of evil. His explanation in dialogue with Valentinian is extensive and intricate. But his conclusion is simple and beneficial. It will be presented in three parts.)

God created nothing that is by nature evil. Evil did not exist as a reality independent of God and in conflict with him. Only by abuse and misuse of the good things God created did evil come into existence. God created humans, giving them the gift of free will, including the power to obey or disobey the Creator. This is the meaning of God's gift of freedom. After God created humans, he gave them his commandment. Evil arose because humans chose to disobey God's will and abuse his gift. This alone is the source of evil in the world. Humans were endowed with the power of freedom so that they might willingly obey their Creator. Through disobedience, humans became enslaved, not because they were overpowered by irresistible tendencies in their created nature or because the capacity with which they were endowed was inadequate for choosing the best.

METHODIUS, *CONCERNING FREE WILL*, A DIALOGUE BETWEEN ORTHODOXUS AND VALENTINIAN

PRAISE THE LORD, for he is glorious;
Never shall his promise fail.
God hath made his saints victorious;
Sin and death shall not prevail.
Praise the God of our salvation;
Hosts on high, his power proclaim.
Heaven and earth and all creation,
Laud and magnify his name. Amen.

ANONYMOUS (CA. 1801), HYMNARY

FOR REFLECTION: Gen. 3:1-17; Ps. 37:1; Prov. 11:1-9; Jer. 13:33; Rom. 14:12

161

God endowed humans with freedom so they could obtain a greater good in addition to the initial gift of freedom. If humans had been created like mere members of the natural world, they would have rendered service to God in a similar way. They would have been mere instruments of the Maker and would not have had the capacity to obtain a good that befits deliberate choice. And it would have been unreasonable for humans to suffer blame for wrongdoing, for they would not have had the option of freely choosing better things. But God, wanting to honor humans and to grant them understanding of better things, has given the power of freedom. He commends the employment of that gift for achieving better things. But God doesn't accomplish this by depriving humans of free will. Instead, he exhorts humans to use their power of choice to obtain better things.

METHODIUS, *CONCERNING FREE WILL,* A DIALOGUE BETWEEN
ORTHODOXUS AND VALENTINIAN

HOLY ARE YOU, King of eternity and Lord and Giver of all holiness; holy also is your only begotten Son, our Lord Jesus Christ, by whom you have made all things; holy also is your Holy Spirit, who searches all things, even your deep things, O God. You made man from earth after your own image and likeness and gave him the joy of paradise, and when he transgressed your commandment and fell away, you did not disregard or desert him, O Good One, but chastened him as a merciful father, called him by the law, instructed him by the prophets, and afterward sent forth your only begotten Son himself, our Lord Jesus Christ, into the world, that the Son by his coming might renew and restore your image. To the all-merciful and gracious God, be praise and thanksgiving, now, always, and forever. Amen.

THE DIVINE LITURGY OF JAMES THE HOLY APOSTLE (CA. AD 150–200)

FOR REFLECTION: Josh. 24:14-18; Matt. 11:28; 23:27; John 1:12; 3:16; Acts 9:20-23; 26:19-32; Heb. 3:12–4:2; 2 Pet. 3:9

162

When God created humans, he did not do so poorly. He did not need to repent of a blunder as a poor craftsman might do. Nor did God intend to create angels and, by mistake, end up creating humans. That would have been a sign of weakness. For why would God have created humans if his intention was to create angels? Was he unable? It would be blasphemous to suppose so. Or maybe when making humans, God lazily made something inferior when he could just as easily have made something superior. This, too, is absurd. For God never fails to create the good; nor does he delay doing so.

God has the power to act when and how he pleases. The reason God created humankind is because that is exactly what he intended to create. But if that is what God intended, and if what God makes is good, then humankind was good when created by God. Now God created humankind as body and soul. Humans cannot therefore be complete without a body. When at the resurrection of the body, Christians rise and lay aside mortality of the flesh, then the body will be freed from corruption and will be subject no longer to vanity but to righteousness alone.

METHODIUS, *FROM THE DISCOURSE ON THE RESURRECTION*, PT. 1, PARAS. 8, 11

ALMIGHTY GOD, who created us in your image: Grant us grace fearlessly to contend against evil and to make no peace with oppression; and, that we may reverently use our freedom, help us to employ it in the maintenance of justice in our communities and among the nations, to the glory of your holy name; through Jesus Christ our Lord, who lives and reigns with you and the Holy Spirit, one God, now and forever. Amen.

"FOR SOCIAL JUSTICE," COLLECTS: CONTEMPORARY, IN BCP

FOR REFLECTION: Gen. 1:26-28; Ps. 33:1-22; Isa. 42:5-11; Acts 17:22-31; 1 Cor. 6:14-15; 15:45-57; 2 Cor. 4:11-18

163

The Son of God does nothing needlessly. He did not take the form of a human servant without reason but to raise it up and save it, for he truly was made man and died—not in mere appearance, but truly—so that he might become the first begotten from the dead. Now he can transform the earthly into the heavenly, and mortality into immortality. If the kingdom of God could be overcome by the corruptible, then the corruptible would take control of incorruption. If the kingdom of God, which is eternal life, could be controlled by the corruptible body, it would happen that life would be consumed by corruption. But now the kingdom of God takes charge of what is perishing so that "death may be swallowed up in victory" and the corruptible may be seen to be the possession of incorruption and immortality. Death is now the servant of immortality; the body is the possession of incorruption, not incorruption the possession of corruption.

METHODIUS, *FROM THE DISCOURSE ON THE RESURRECTION*, PT. 1, PARA. 13

HAIL TO THE LORD'S ANOINTED,
Great David's greater Son!
Hail in the time appointed,
His reign on earth begun!
He comes to break oppression,
To set the captive free,
To take away transgression
And rule in equity. Amen.

JAMES MONTGOMERY (1771–1854), HYMNARY

FOR REFLECTION: Rom. 3:19-25; 5:1-21; **1 Cor. 15:3-58**; Rev. 7:9-17; 12:10-17

APPENDIX

✛

A LIST OF THE ANTE-NICENE FATHERS

The Apostolic Fathers

Clement of Rome (ca. AD 30-100)

The *Teaching of the Twelve Apostles* (*Didache*) (ca. AD 70–150)

Ignatius of Antioch (called Theophorus [God-bearer]) (ca. AD 50–ca. 98-117)

Polycarp of Smyrna (ca. AD 69–ca. 156)

Papias of Hierapolis (fl. first quarter of the second century AD)

The *Epistle of Barnabas* (so-called) (ca. AD 135)

The *Shepherd of Hermas* (ca. AD 100-160)

The *Epistle to Diognetus* (*Mathetes*) (ca. AD 130)

The Apologists

Quadratus (d. ca. AD 129)

Aristides of Athens (ca. AD 140)

Aristo of Pella (ca. AD 140)

Miltiades (fl. AD 160-93)

Claudius Apollinarius, bishop of Hierapolis in Phrygia (fl. ca. AD 160-80)

Melito, bishop of Sardis (fl. ca. AD 160-80)

Justin Martyr (ca. 100–ca. AD 165)

Tatian (ca. AD 120-80)

Athenagoras "the Philosopher" (ca. AD 133-90)

Theophilus of Antioch (d. ca. AD 183-85)

The Second- and Third-Century Fathers

Irenaeus (d. ca. AD 202)

Clement of Alexandria (d. ca. AD 215)

Hippolytus of Rome (ca. AD 170–235)

Tertullian (ca. AD 160–ca. 225)

Minucius Felix (late second and early third centuries AD)

Commodian (Commodianus) (fl. ca. AD 250)

Origen (ca. AD 185–ca. 254)

Cyprian of Carthage (ca. AD 210-58)

Caius (early third century AD)

Novatian (ca. AD 200-ca. 258)

Gregory the Wonder-Worker (Gregory Thaumaturgus, Gregory of Neocaesarea) (ca. AD 213-ca. 270)

Dionysius of Alexandria (Dionysius the Great) (ca. AD 190–265)

Julius Africanus (ca. AD 160–ca. 240)

Anatolius of Laodicea (Anatolius of Alexandria) (d. ca. AD 282)

Methodius (d. ca. AD 311)

Arnobius (d. ca. AD 330)

The Fourth-Century Fathers before Nicaea

Lactantius (ca. AD 240–ca. 320)

Victorinus, bishop of Pettau, Austria (d. ca. AD 304)

Pamphilus, bishop of Caesarea (martyred in AD 309)

SOURCES

The reading, prayers, and hymns used in this book were adapted from the following sources:

Ante-Nicene Fathers. 10 vols. Reprint of the 1885 edition, Christian Classics Ethereal Library. http://www.ccel.org/fathers.html.

Apostolic Fathers. Translated by J. B. Lightfoot. Edited and completed by J. R. Harmer. 1891. Reprint of 1956 Baker Book House edition, Christian Classics Ethereal Library. http://www.ccel.org/ccel/lightfoot/fathers.titlepage.html.

Book of Common Prayer. New York: Church Hymnal Corporation, 1979. http://justus.anglican.org/resources/bcp/formatted _1979.htm.

Book of Common Prayer for Scotland. 1637. http://justus.anglican .org/resources/bcp/Scotland/BCP_1637.htm.

A Collection of Hymns for the Use of the People Called Methodists. 1889. http://www.ccel.org/w/wesley/hymn/jw.html#index.

Hymnary.org. http://www.hymnary.org/texts?qu=+in:texts.

Scottish Book of Common Prayer. 1929. http://justus.anglican.org/ resources/bcp/Scotland/Scot_Collects_Epistles_Gospels.htm.

Sing to the Lord. Kansas City: Lillenas Publishing Company, 1993.